KING

2

Written and Illustrated by
HO CHE ANDERSON

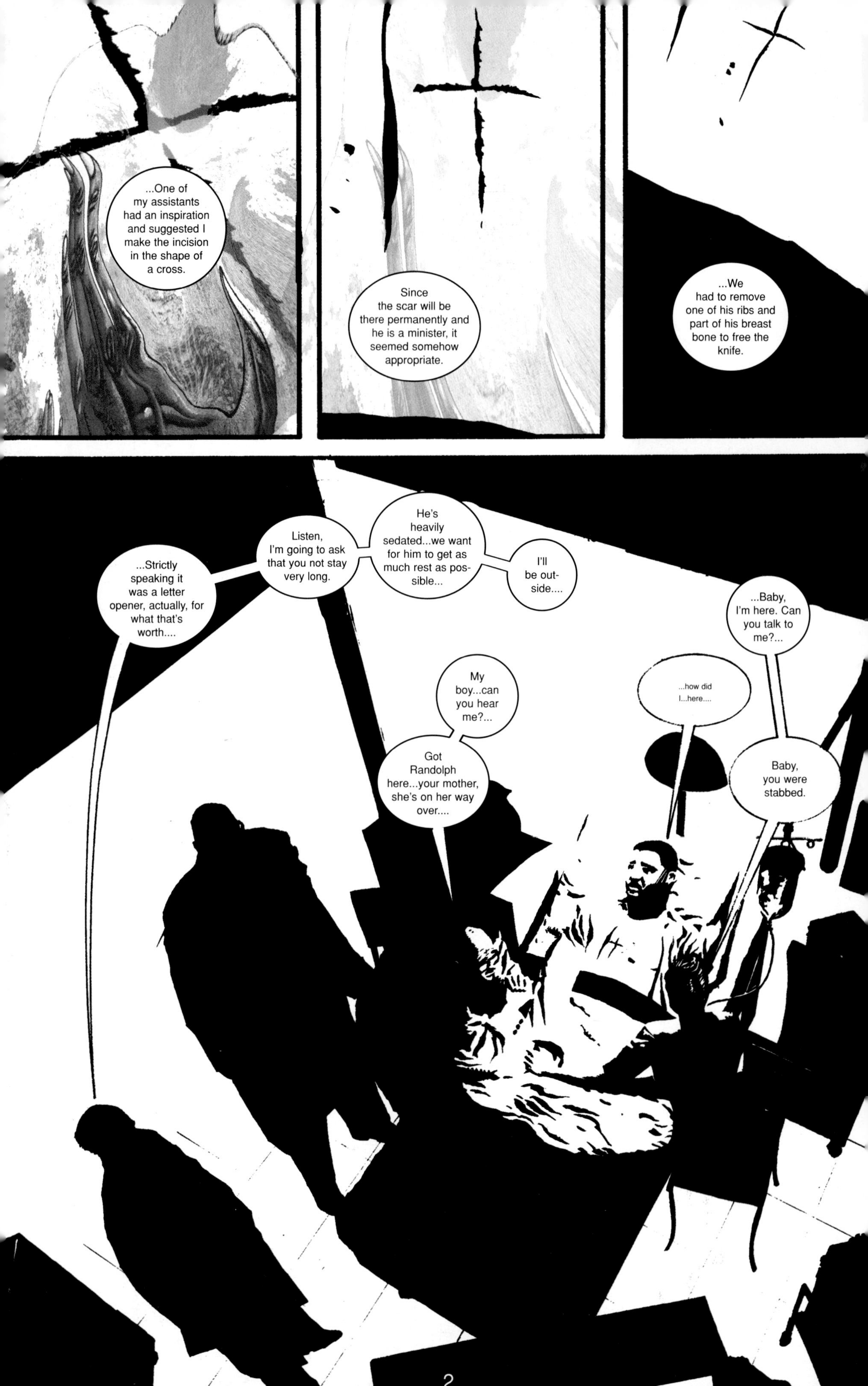
...One of my assistants had an inspiration and suggested I make the incision in the shape of a cross.
Since the scar will be there permanently and he is a minister, it seemed somehow appropriate.
...We had to remove one of his ribs and part of his breast bone to free the knife.
...Strictly speaking it was a letter opener, actually, for what that's worth....
Listen, I'm going to ask that you not stay very long.
He's heavily sedated...we want for him to get as much rest as possible...
I'll be outside....
...Baby, I'm here. Can you talk to me?...
My boy...can you hear me?...
Got Randolph here...your mother, she's on her way over....
...how did I...here....
Baby, you were stabbed.

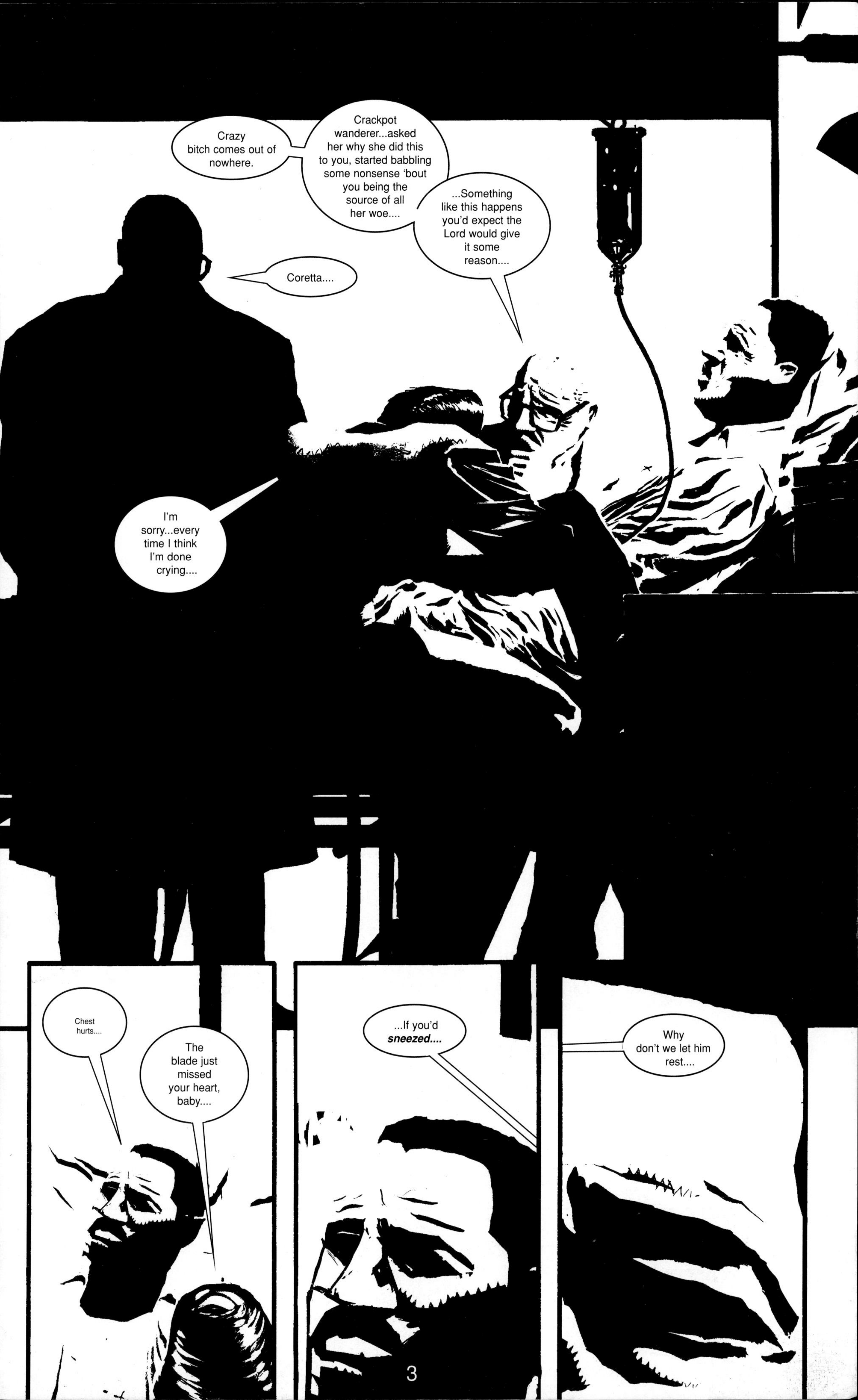
Crazy bitch comes out of nowhere.
Crackpot wanderer...asked her why she did this to you, started babbling some nonsense 'bout you being the source of all her woe....
...Something like this happens you'd expect the Lord would give it some reason....
Coretta....
I'm sorry...every time I think I'm done crying....
Chest hurts....
The blade just missed your heart, baby....
...If you'd ***sneezed....***
Why don't we let him rest....

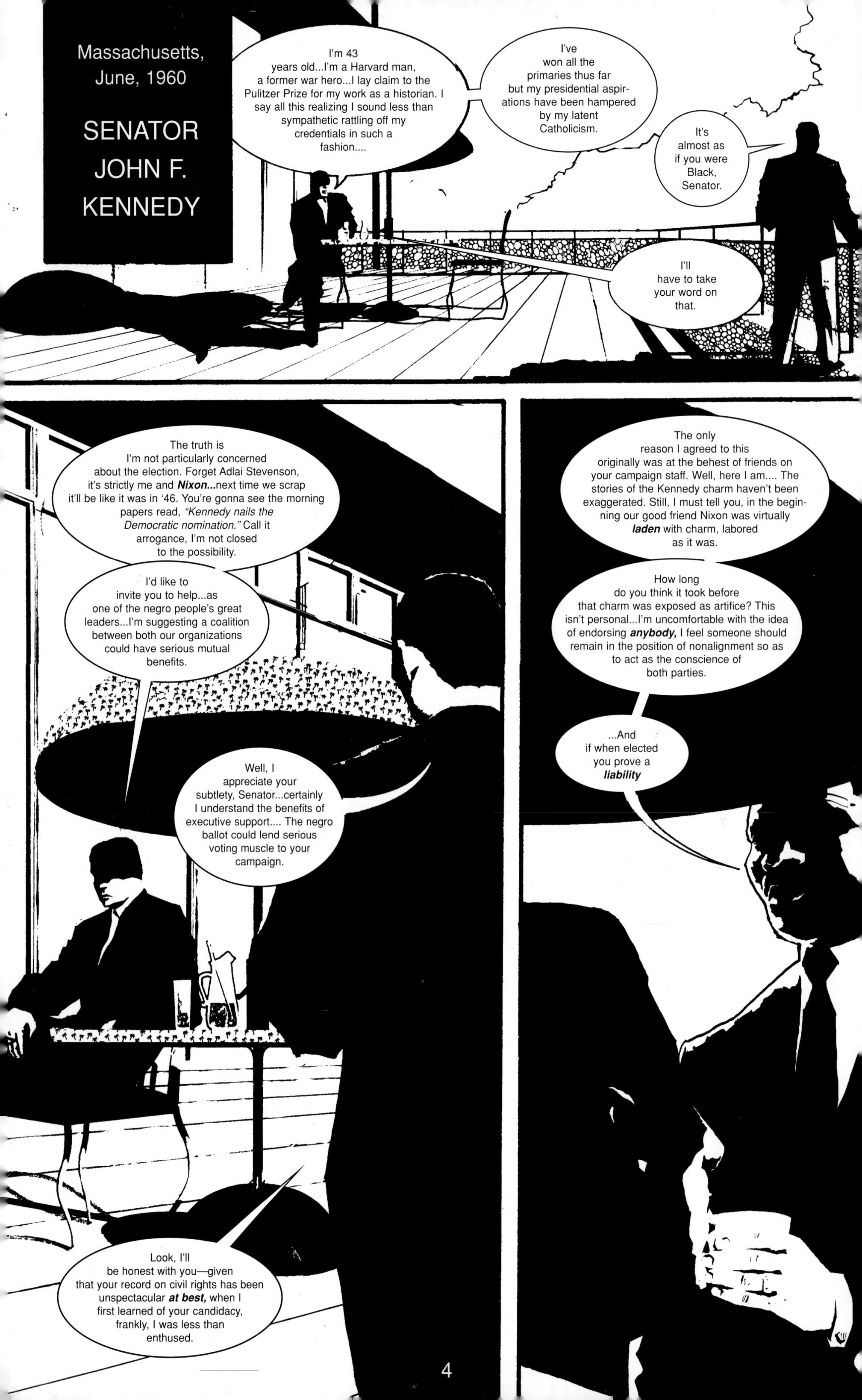
Massachusetts, June, 1960
SENATOR JOHN F. KENNEDY
I'm 43 years old...I'm a Harvard man, a former war hero...I lay claim to the Pulitzer Prize for my work as a historian. I say all this realizing I sound less than sympathetic rattling off my credentials in such a fashion....
I've won all the primaries thus far but my presidential aspirations have been hampered by my latent Catholicism.
It's almost as if you were Black, Senator.
I'll have to take your word on that.
The truth is I'm not particularly concerned about the election. Forget Adlai Stevenson, it's strictly me and ***Nixon...*** next time we scrap it'll be like it was in '46. You're gonna see the morning papers read, *"Kennedy nails the Democratic nomination."* Call it arrogance, I'm not closed to the possibility.
I'd like to invite you to help...as one of the negro people's great leaders...I'm suggesting a coalition between both our organizations could have serious mutual benefits.
Well, I appreciate your subtlety, Senator...certainly I understand the benefits of executive support.... The negro ballot could lend serious voting muscle to your campaign.
Look, I'll be honest with you—given that your record on civil rights has been unspectacular ***at best,*** when I first learned of your candidacy, frankly, I was less than enthused.
The only reason I agreed to this originally was at the behest of friends on your campaign staff. Well, here I am.... The stories of the Kennedy charm haven't been exaggerated. Still, I must tell you, in the beginning our good friend Nixon was virtually ***laden*** with charm, labored as it was.
How long do you think it took before that charm was exposed as artifice? This isn't personal...I'm uncomfortable with the idea of endorsing ***anybody,*** I feel someone should remain in the position of nonalignment so as to act as the conscience of both parties.
...And if when elected you prove a ***liability***

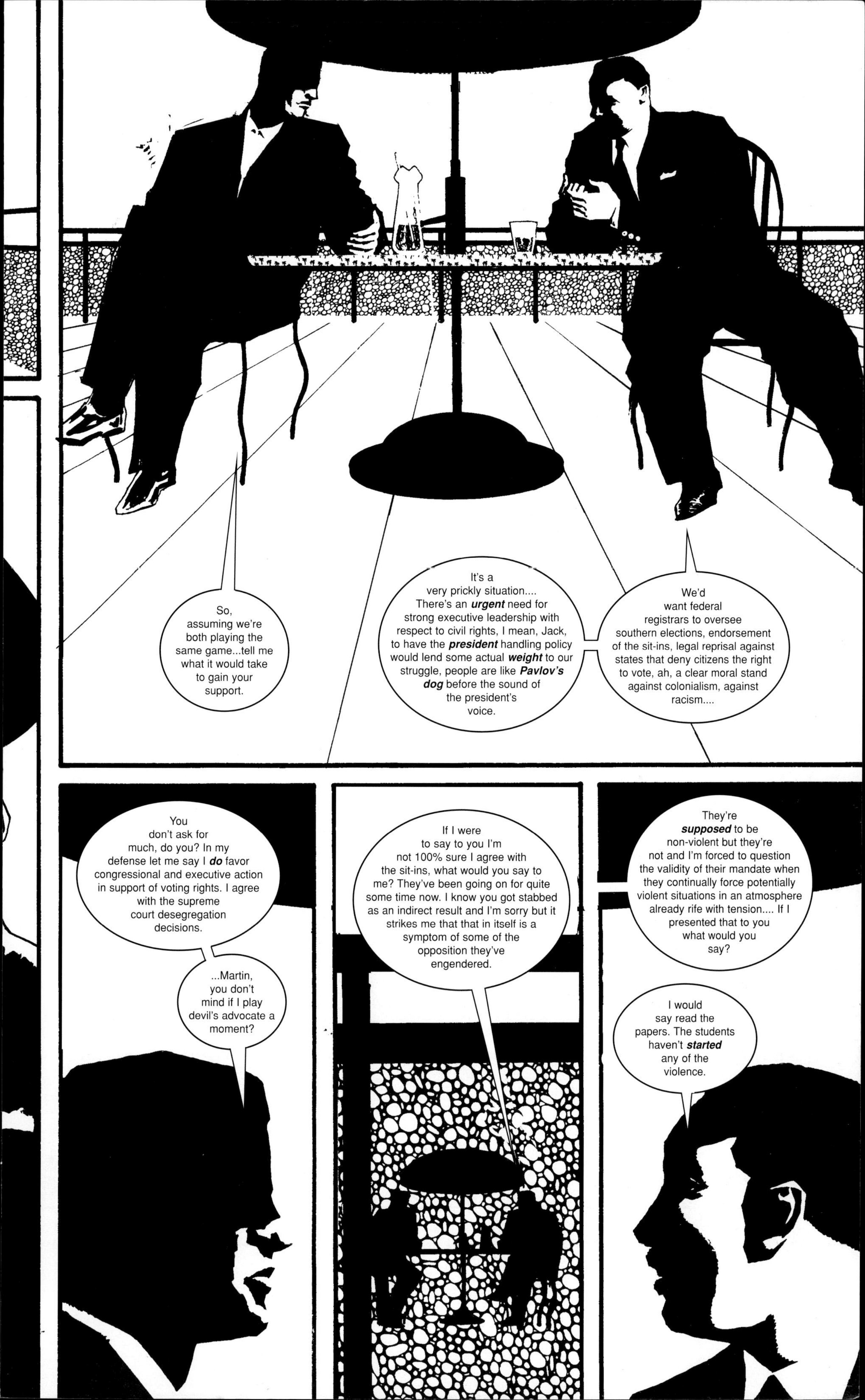
So, assuming we're both playing the same game...tell me what it would take to gain your support.
It's a very prickly situation.... There's an *urgent* need for strong executive leadership with respect to civil rights, I mean, Jack, to have the *president* handling policy would lend some actual *weight* to our struggle, people are like *Pavlov's dog* before the sound of the president's voice.
We'd want federal registrars to oversee southern elections, endorsement of the sit-ins, legal reprisal against states that deny citizens the right to vote, ah, a clear moral stand against colonialism, against racism....
You don't ask for much, do you? In my defense let me say I *do* favor congressional and executive action in support of voting rights. I agree with the supreme court desegregation decisions.
...Martin, you don't mind if I play devil's advocate a moment?
If I were to say to you I'm not 100% sure I agree with the sit-ins, what would you say to me? They've been going on for quite some time now. I know you got stabbed as an indirect result and I'm sorry but it strikes me that that in itself is a symptom of some of the opposition they've engendered.
They're *supposed* to be non-violent but they're not and I'm forced to question the validity of their mandate when they continually force potentially violent situations in an atmosphere already rife with tension.... If I presented that to you what would you say?
I would say read the papers. The students haven't *started* any of the violence.

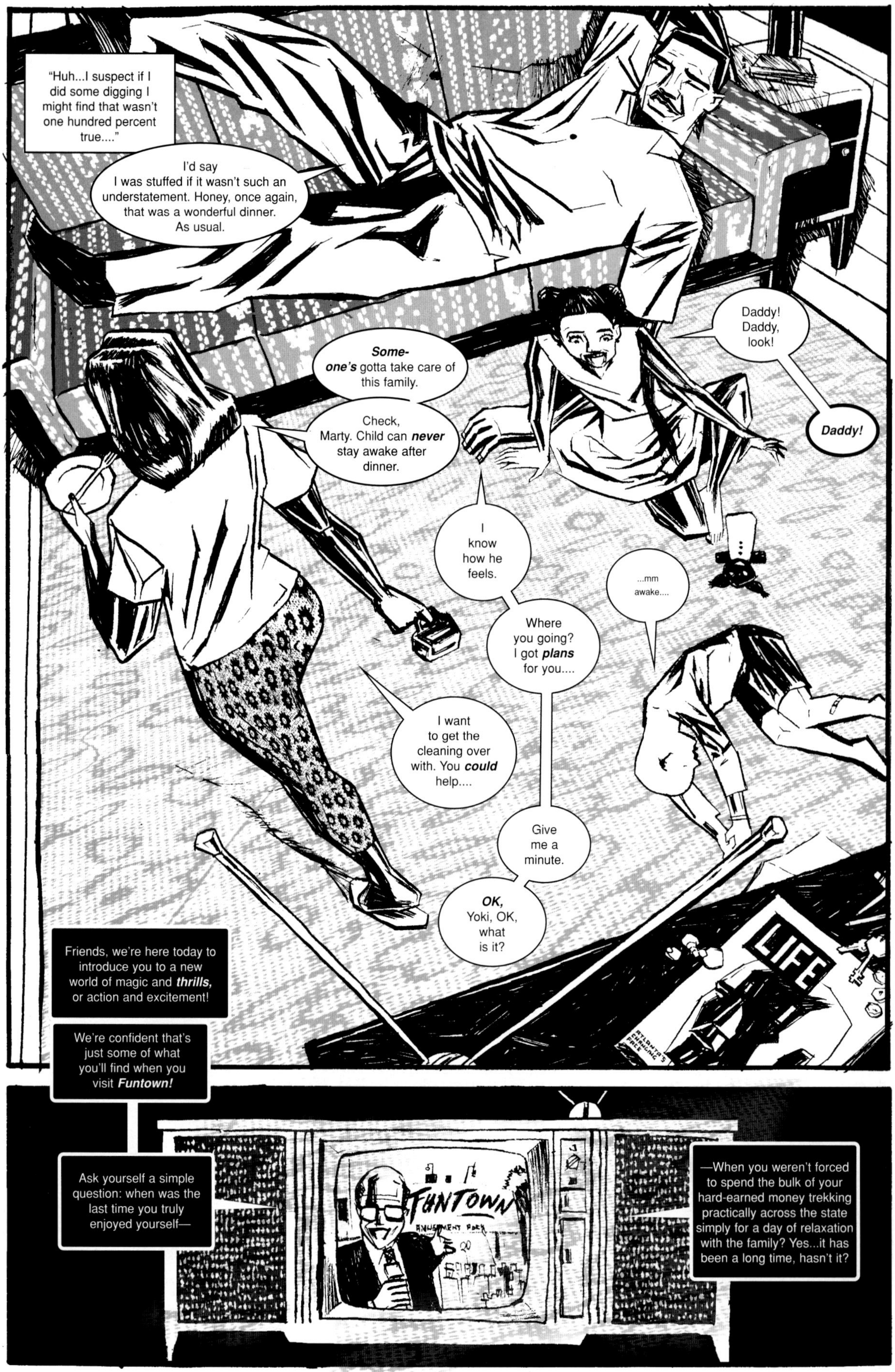
"Huh...I suspect if I did some digging I might find that wasn't one hundred percent true...."
I'd say I was stuffed if it wasn't such an understatement. Honey, once again, that was a wonderful dinner. As usual.
Some-one's gotta take care of this family.
Check, Marty. Child can ***never*** stay awake after dinner.
Daddy! Daddy, look!
Daddy!
I know how he feels.
Where you going? I got ***plans*** for you....
...mm awake....
I want to get the cleaning over with. You ***could*** help....
Give me a minute.
OK, Yoki, OK, what is it?
LIFE
Friends, we're here today to introduce you to a new world of magic and ***thrills,*** or action and excitement!
We're confident that's just some of what you'll find when you visit ***Funtown!***
FUNTOWN
AMUSEMENT PARK
Ask yourself a simple question: when was the last time you truly enjoyed yourself—
—When you weren't forced to spend the bulk of your hard-earned money trekking practically across the state simply for a day of relaxation with the family? Yes...it has been a long time, hasn't it?

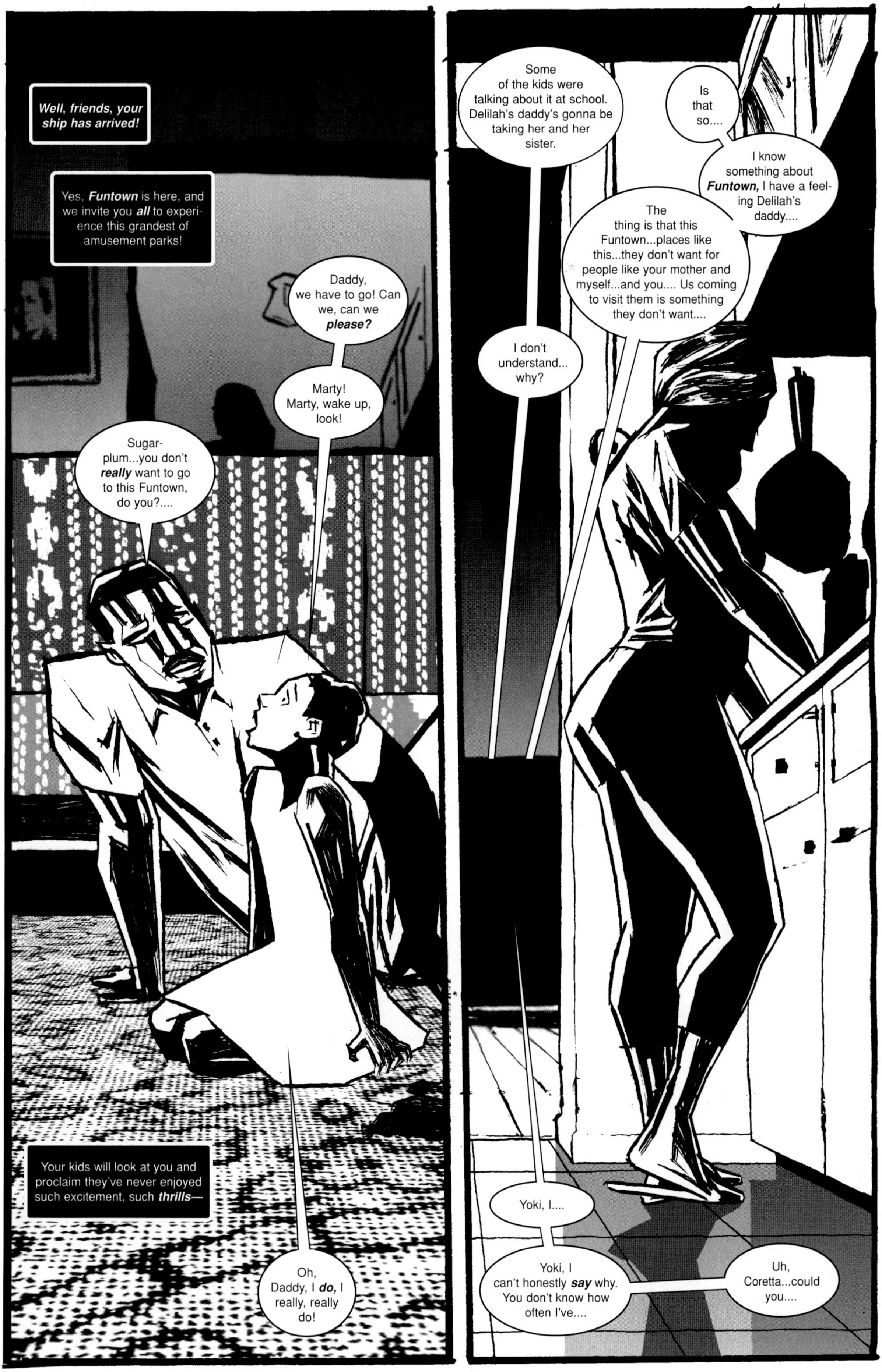

Well, friends, your ship has arrived!
Yes, ***Funtown*** is here, and we invite you ***all*** to experience this grandest of amusement parks!
Daddy, we have to go! Can we, can we ***please?***
Marty! Marty, wake up, look!
Sugar-plum...you don't ***really*** want to go to this Funtown, do you?....
Your kids will look at you and proclaim they've never enjoyed such excitement, such ***thrills—***
Oh, Daddy, I ***do,*** I really, really do!
Some of the kids were talking about it at school. Delilah's daddy's gonna be taking her and her sister.
Is that so....
I know something about ***Funtown,*** I have a feeling Delilah's daddy....
The thing is that this Funtown...places like this...they don't want for people like your mother and myself...and you.... Us coming to visit them is something they don't want....
I don't understand... why?
Yoki, I....
Yoki, I can't honestly ***say*** why. You don't know how often I've....
Uh, Coretta...could you....

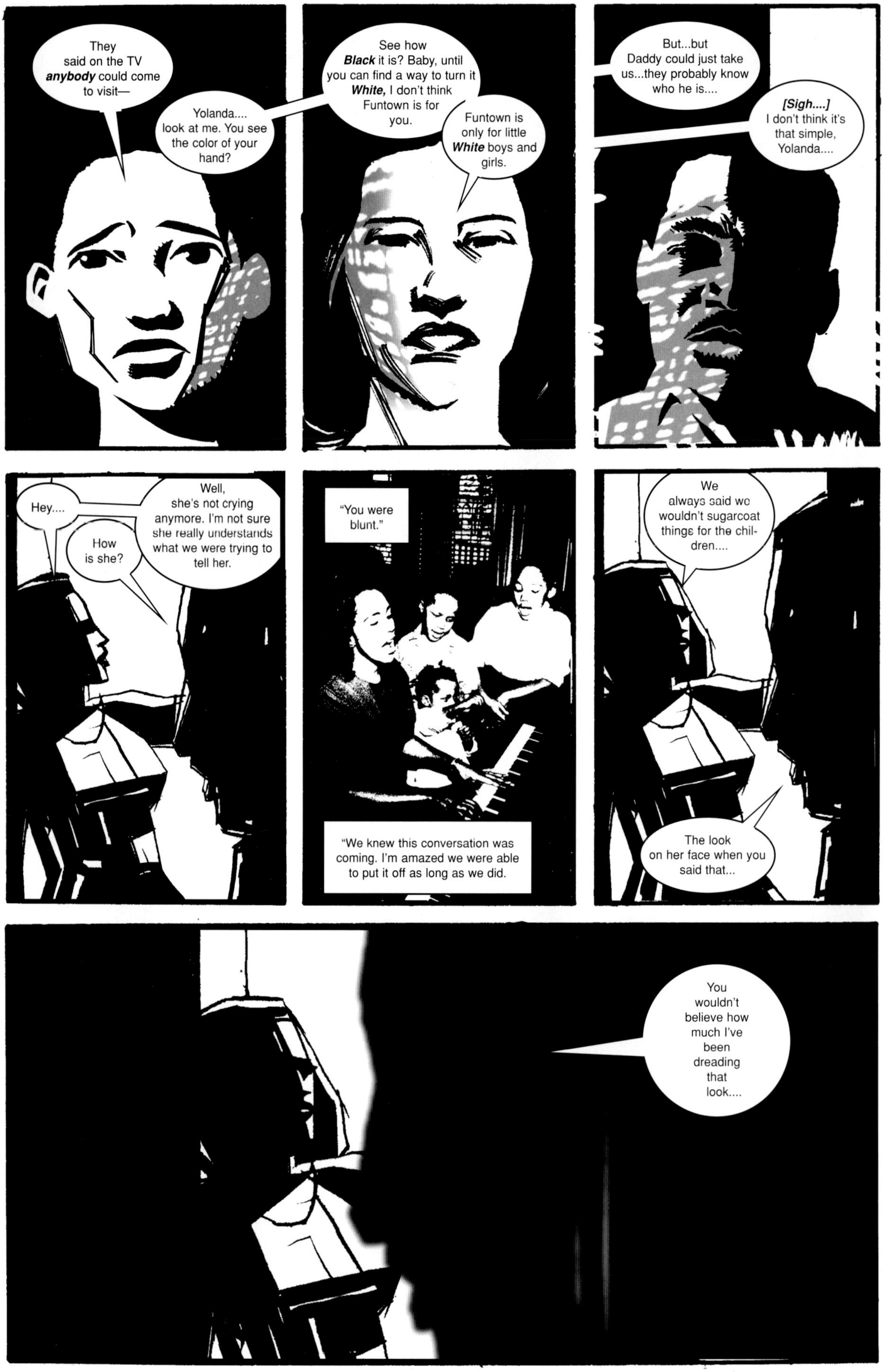
They said on the TV *anybody* could come to visit—
Yolanda.... look at me. You see the color of your hand?
See how *Black* it is? Baby, until you can find a way to turn it *White,* I don't think Funtown is for you.
Funtown is only for little *White* boys and girls.
But...but Daddy could just take us...they probably know who he is....
[Sigh....] I don't think it's that simple, Yolanda....
Hey....
How is she?
Well, she's not crying anymore. I'm not sure she really understands what we were trying to tell her.
"You were blunt."
"We knew this conversation was coming. I'm amazed we were able to put it off as long as we did.
We always said we wouldn't sugarcoat things for the children....
The look on her face when you said that...
You wouldn't believe how much I've been dreading that look....

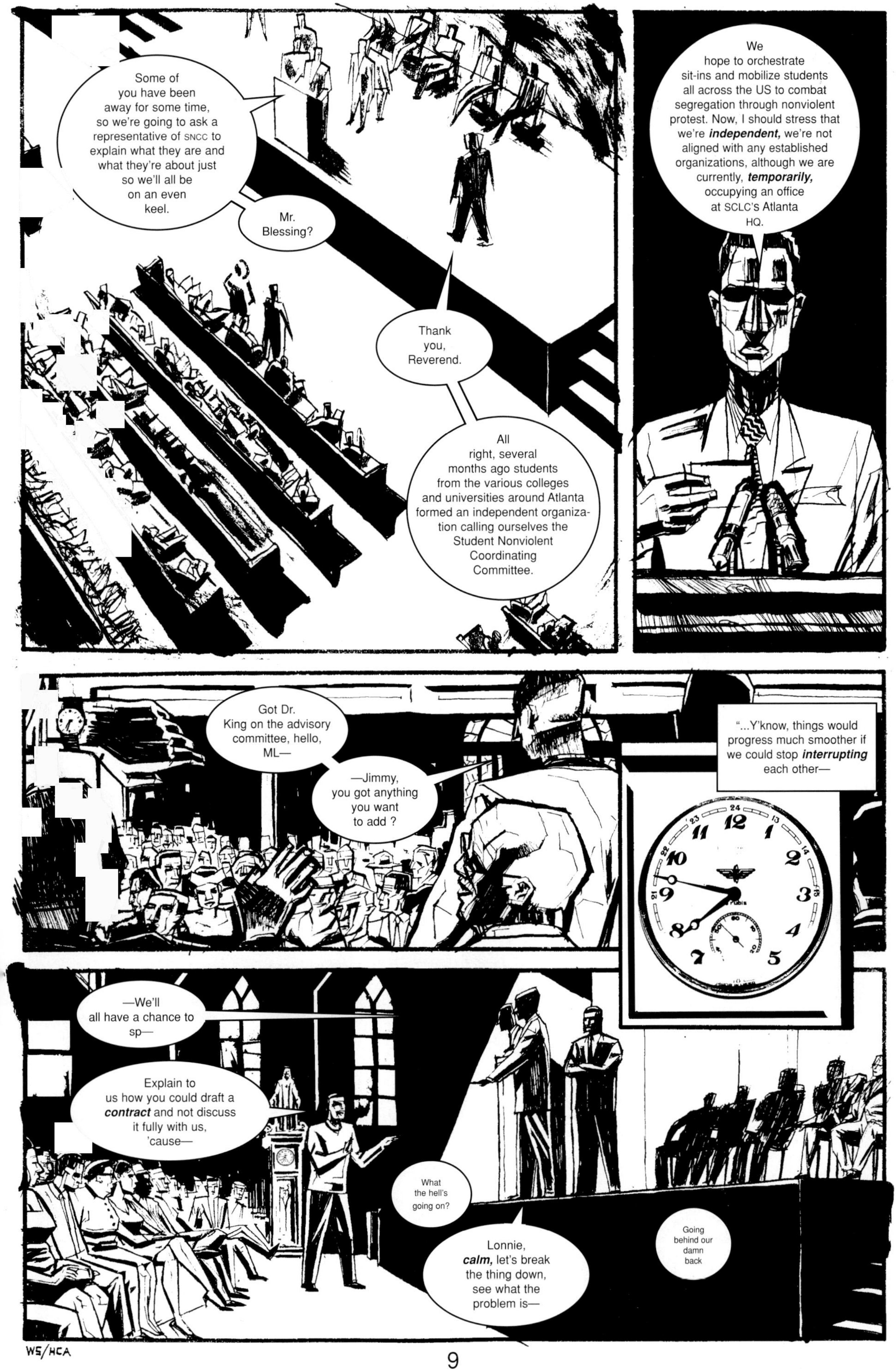
Some of you have been away for some time, so we're going to ask a representative of SNCC to explain what they are and what they're about just so we'll all be on an even keel.
Mr. Blessing?
Thank you, Reverend.
All right, several months ago students from the various colleges and universities around Atlanta formed an independent organization calling ourselves the Student Nonviolent Coordinating Committee.
We hope to orchestrate sit-ins and mobilize students all across the US to combat segregation through nonviolent protest. Now, I should stress that we're ***independent,*** we're not aligned with any established organizations, although we are currently, ***temporarily,*** occupying an office at SCLC's Atlanta HQ.
Got Dr. King on the advisory committee, hello, ML—
—Jimmy, you got anything you want to add ?
"...Y'know, things would progress much smoother if we could stop ***interrupting*** each other—
—We'll all have a chance to sp—
Explain to us how you could draft a ***contract*** and not discuss it fully with us, 'cause—
What the hell's going on?
Lonnie, ***calm,*** let's break the thing down, see what the problem is—
Going behind our damn back
WS/HCA

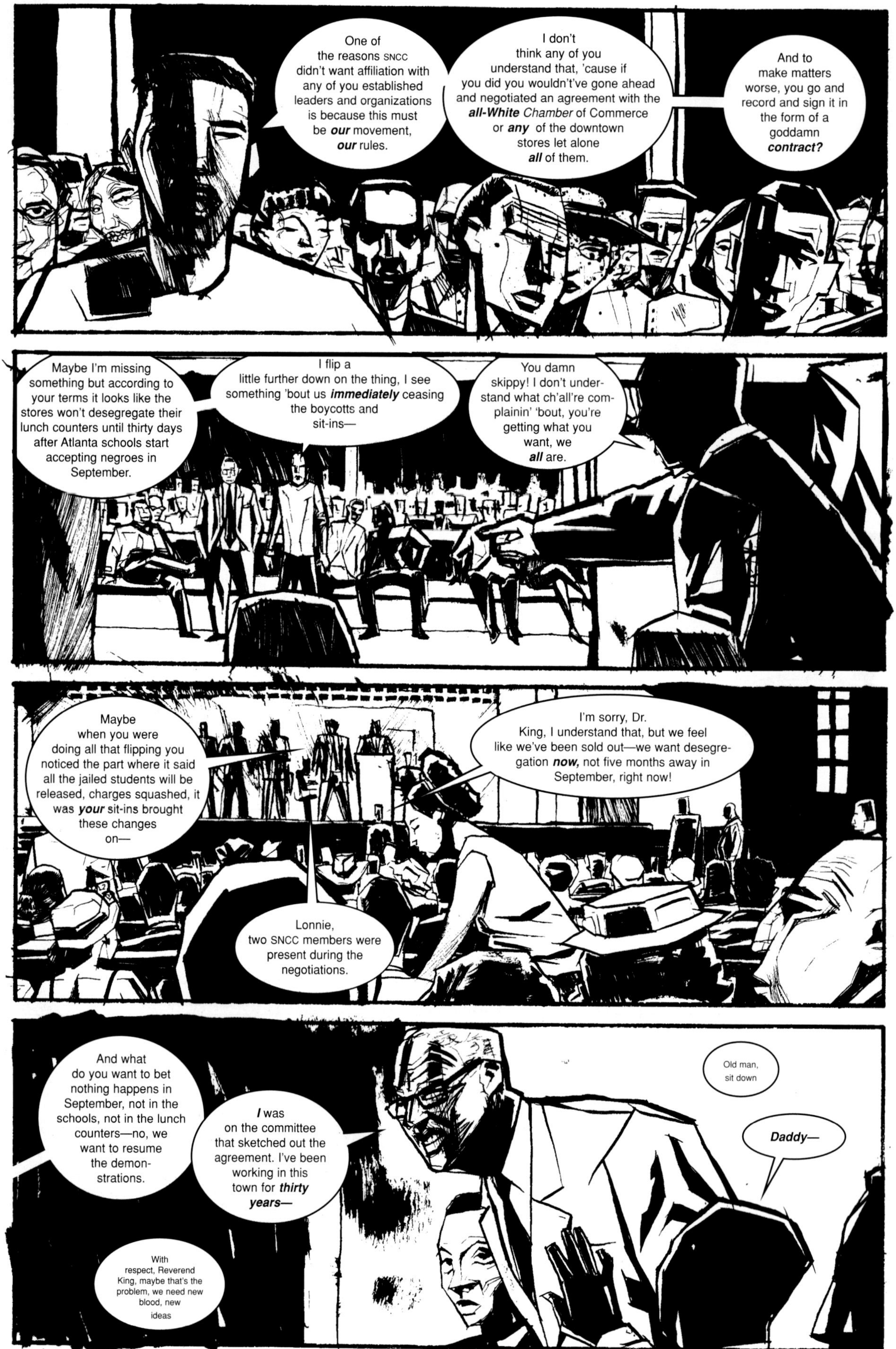
One of the reasons SNCC didn't want affiliation with any of you established leaders and organizations is because this must be ***our*** movement, ***our*** rules.
I don't think any of you understand that, 'cause if you did you wouldn't've gone ahead and negotiated an agreement with the ***all-White*** *Chamber* of Commerce or ***any*** of the downtown stores let alone ***all*** of them.
And to make matters worse, you go and record and sign it in the form of a goddamn ***contract?***
Maybe I'm missing something but according to your terms it looks like the stores won't desegregate their lunch counters until thirty days after Atlanta schools start accepting negroes in September.
I flip a little further down on the thing, I see something 'bout us ***immediately*** ceasing the boycotts and sit-ins—
You damn skippy! I don't understand what ch'all're complainin' 'bout, you're getting what you want, we ***all*** are.
Maybe when you were doing all that flipping you noticed the part where it said all the jailed students will be released, charges squashed, it was ***your*** sit-ins brought these changes on—
I'm sorry, Dr. King, I understand that, but we feel like we've been sold out—we want desegregation ***now,*** not five months away in September, right now!
Lonnie, two SNCC members were present during the negotiations.
And what do you want to bet nothing happens in September, not in the schools, not in the lunch counters—no, we want to resume the demonstrations.
I was on the committee that sketched out the agreement. I've been working in this town for ***thirty years—***
Old man, sit down
Daddy—
With respect, Reverend King, maybe that's the problem, we need new blood, new ideas
WS/HCA

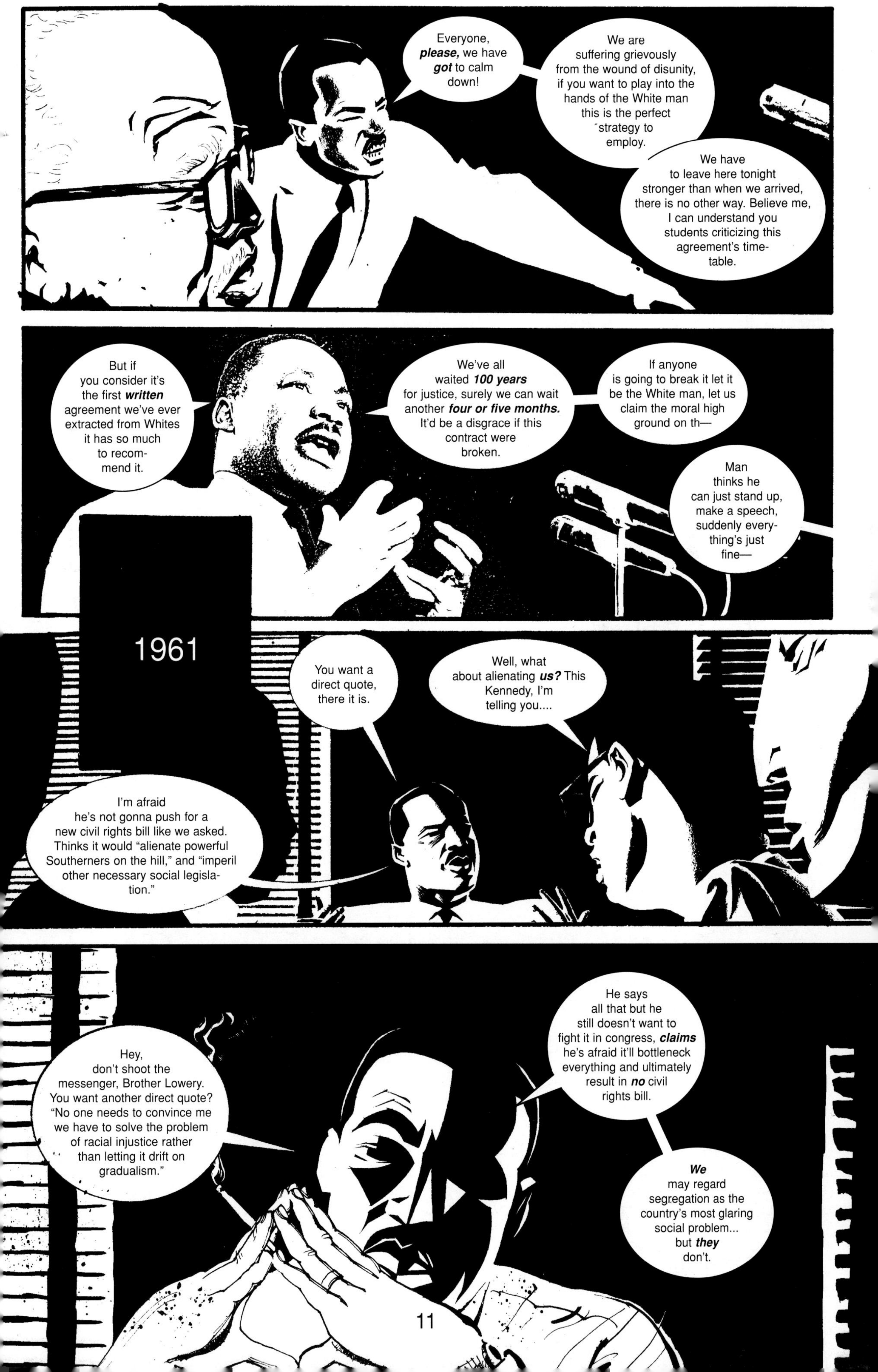
Everyone, please, we have got to calm down!
We are suffering grievously from the wound of disunity, if you want to play into the hands of the White man this is the perfect strategy to employ.
We have to leave here tonight stronger than when we arrived, there is no other way. Believe me, I can understand you students criticizing this agreement's timetable.
But if you consider it's the first written agreement we've ever extracted from Whites it has so much to recommend it.
We've all waited 100 years for justice, surely we can wait another four or five months. It'd be a disgrace if this contract were broken.
If anyone is going to break it let it be the White man, let us claim the moral high ground on th—
Man thinks he can just stand up, make a speech, suddenly everything's just fine—
1961
I'm afraid he's not gonna push for a new civil rights bill like we asked. Thinks it would "alienate powerful Southerners on the hill," and "imperil other necessary social legislation."
You want a direct quote, there it is.
Well, what about alienating us? This Kennedy, I'm telling you....
Hey, don't shoot the messenger, Brother Lowery. You want another direct quote? "No one needs to convince me we have to solve the problem of racial injustice rather than letting it drift on gradualism."
He says all that but he still doesn't want to fight it in congress, claims he's afraid it'll bottleneck everything and ultimately result in no civil rights bill.
We may regard segregation as the country's most glaring social problem... but they don't.

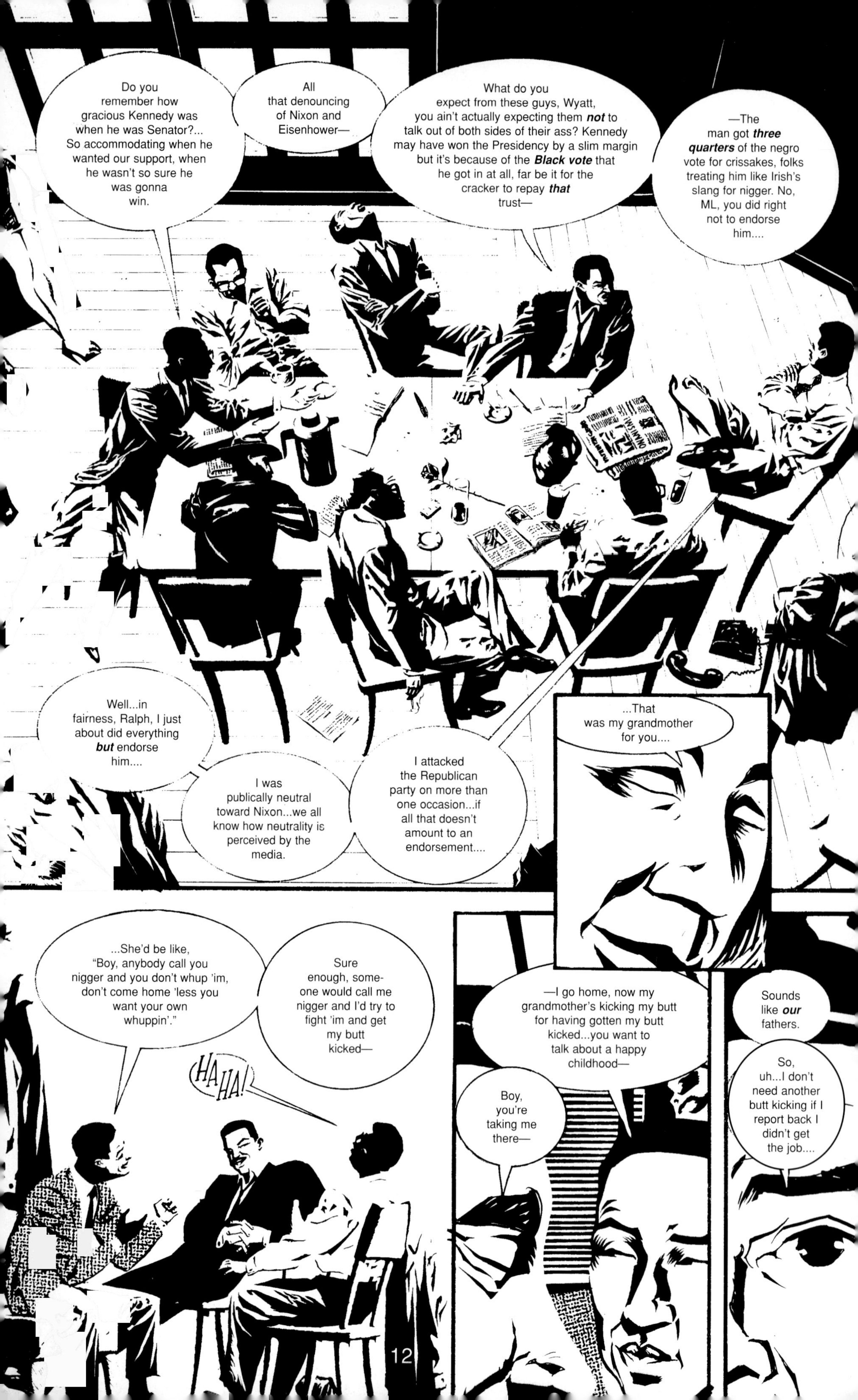

Do you remember how gracious Kennedy was when he was Senator?... So accommodating when he wanted our support, when he wasn't so sure he was gonna win.
All that denouncing of Nixon and Eisenhower—
What do you expect from these guys, Wyatt, you ain't actually expecting them ***not*** to talk out of both sides of their ass? Kennedy may have won the Presidency by a slim margin but it's because of the ***Black vote*** that he got in at all, far be it for the cracker to repay ***that*** trust—
—The man got ***three quarters*** of the negro vote for crissakes, folks treating him like Irish's slang for nigger. No, ML, you did right not to endorse him....
Well...in fairness, Ralph, I just about did everything ***but*** endorse him....
I was publically neutral toward Nixon...we all know how neutrality is perceived by the media.
I attacked the Republican party on more than one occasion...if all that doesn't amount to an endorsement....
...That was my grandmother for you....
...She'd be like, "Boy, anybody call you nigger and you don't whup 'im, don't come home 'less you want your own whuppin'."
Sure enough, some-one would call me nigger and I'd try to fight 'im and get my butt kicked—
HA HA!
—I go home, now my grandmother's kicking my butt for having gotten my butt kicked...you want to talk about a happy childhood—
Boy, you're taking me there—
Sounds like ***our*** fathers.
So, uh...I don't need another butt kicking if I report back I didn't get the job....

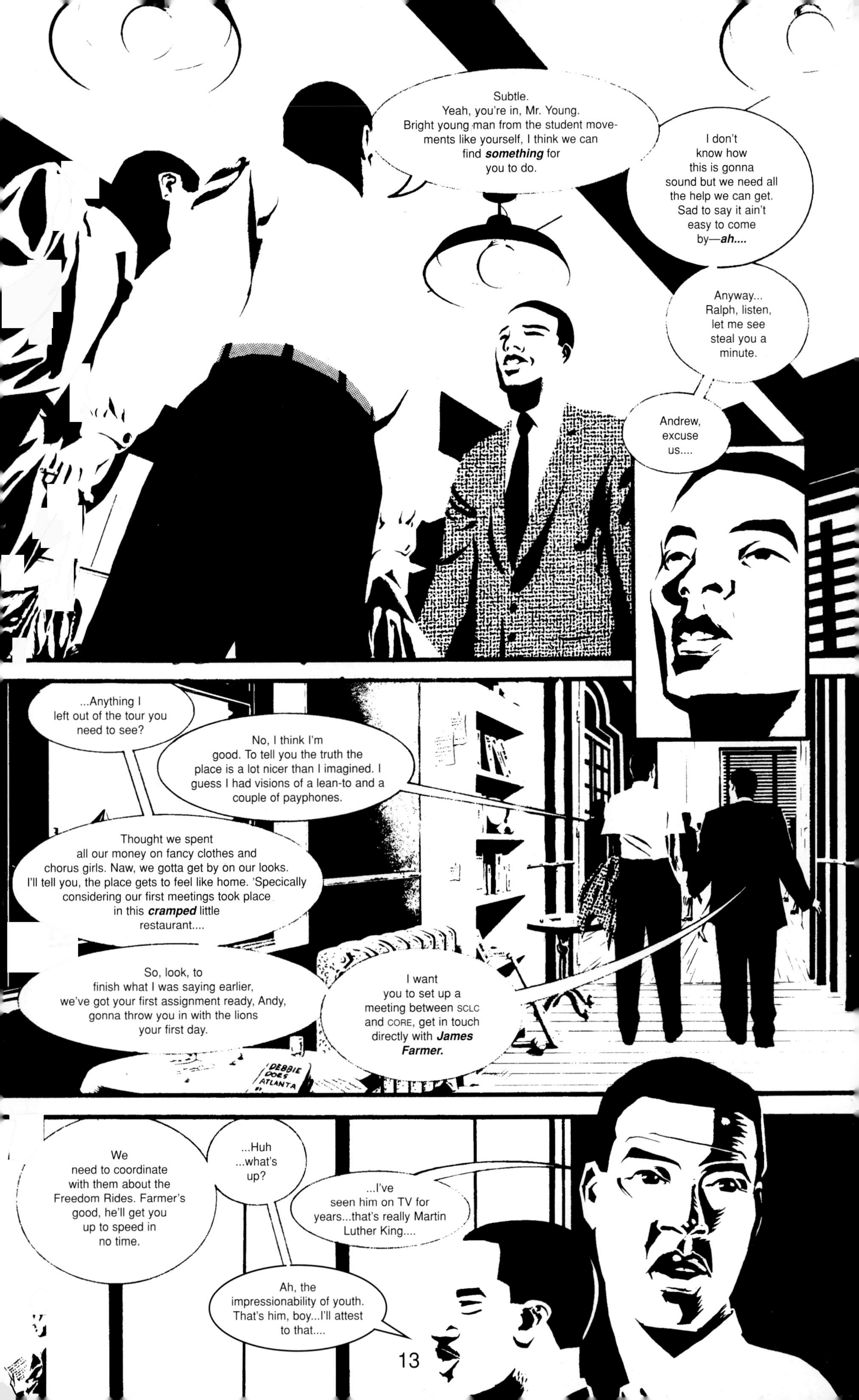

Subtle.
Yeah, you're in, Mr. Young.
Bright young man from the student movements like yourself, I think we can find *something* for you to do.
I don't know how this is gonna sound but we need all the help we can get. Sad to say it ain't easy to come by—*ah....*
Anyway... Ralph, listen, let me see steal you a minute.
Andrew, excuse us....
...Anything I left out of the tour you need to see?
No, I think I'm good. To tell you the truth the place is a lot nicer than I imagined. I guess I had visions of a lean-to and a couple of payphones.
Thought we spent all our money on fancy clothes and chorus girls. Naw, we gotta get by on our looks. I'll tell you, the place gets to feel like home. 'Specically considering our first meetings took place in this *cramped* little restaurant....
So, look, to finish what I was saying earlier, we've got your first assignment ready, Andy, gonna throw you in with the lions your first day.
I want you to set up a meeting between SCLC and CORE, get in touch directly with ***James Farmer.***
DEBBIE DOES ATLANTA
We need to coordinate with them about the Freedom Rides. Farmer's good, he'll get you up to speed in no time.
...Huh ...what's up?
...I've seen him on TV for years...that's really Martin Luther King....
Ah, the impressionability of youth. That's him, boy...I'll attest to that....

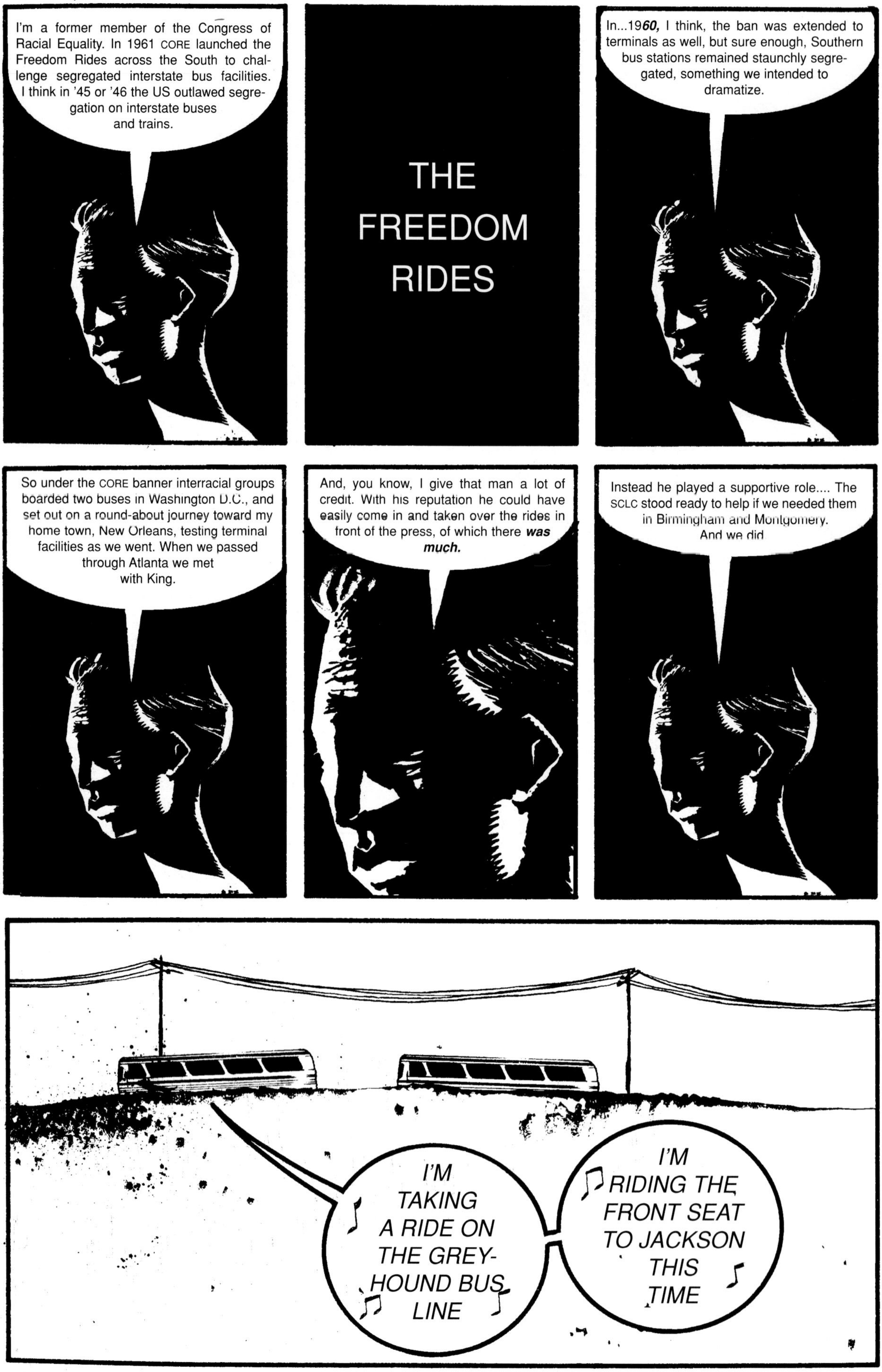
I'm a former member of the Congress of Racial Equality. In 1961 CORE launched the Freedom Rides across the South to challenge segregated interstate bus facilities. I think in '45 or '46 the US outlawed segregation on interstate buses and trains.
THE FREEDOM RIDES
In...19*60,* I think, the ban was extended to terminals as well, but sure enough, Southern bus stations remained staunchly segregated, something we intended to dramatize.
So under the CORE banner interracial groups boarded two buses in Washington D.C., and set out on a round-about journey toward my home town, New Orleans, testing terminal facilities as we went. When we passed through Atlanta we met with King.
And, you know, I give that man a lot of credit. With his reputation he could have easily come in and taken over the rides in front of the press, of which there *was much.*
Instead he played a supportive role.... The SCLC stood ready to help if we needed them in Birmingham and Montgomery. And we did
I'M TAKING A RIDE ON THE GREY-HOUND BUS LINE
I'M RIDING THE FRONT SEAT TO JACKSON THIS TIME

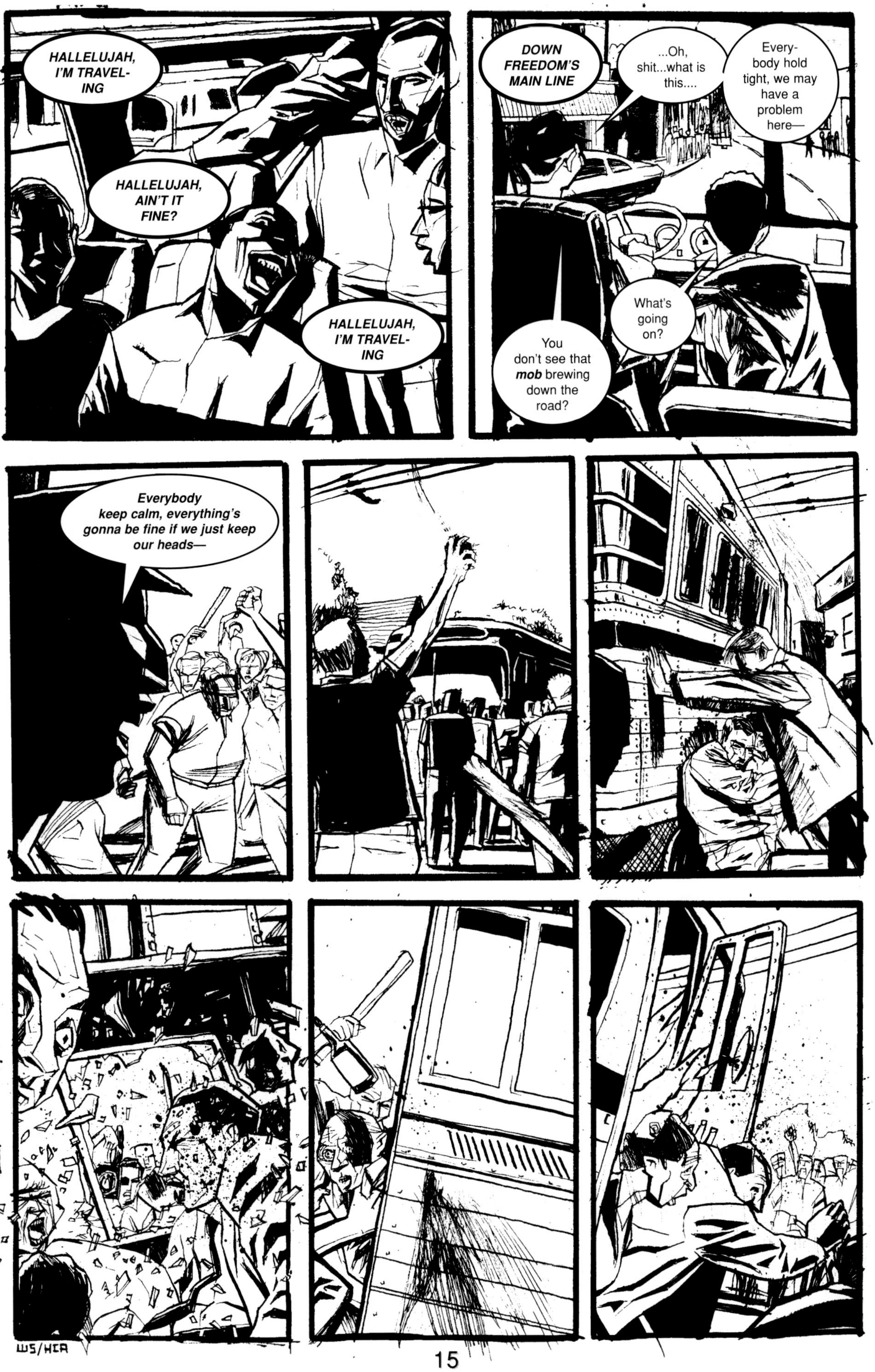
HALLELUJAH, I'M TRAVEL-ING
HALLELUJAH, AIN'T IT FINE?
HALLELUJAH, I'M TRAVEL-ING
DOWN FREEDOM'S MAIN LINE
...Oh, shit...what is this....
Every-body hold tight, we may have a problem here—
You don't see that *mob* brewing down the road?
What's going on?
Everybody keep calm, everything's gonna be fine if we just keep our heads—
WS/HIA

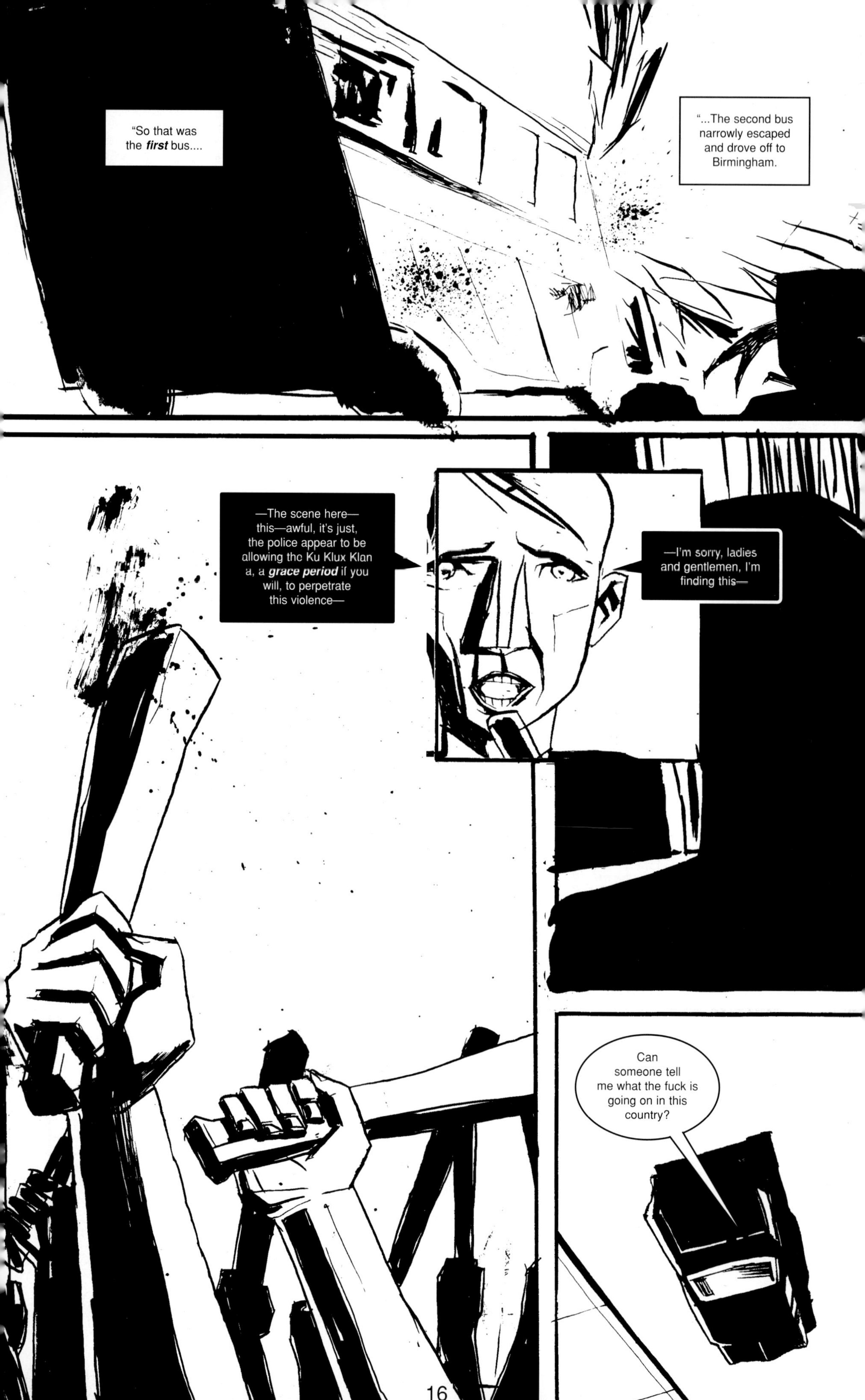
"So that was the *first* bus....
"...The second bus narrowly escaped and drove off to Birmingham.
—The scene here— this—awful, it's just, the police appear to be allowing the Ku Klux Klan a, a *grace period* if you will, to perpetrate this violence—
—I'm sorry, ladies and gentlemen, I'm finding this—
Can someone tell me what the fuck is going on in this country?

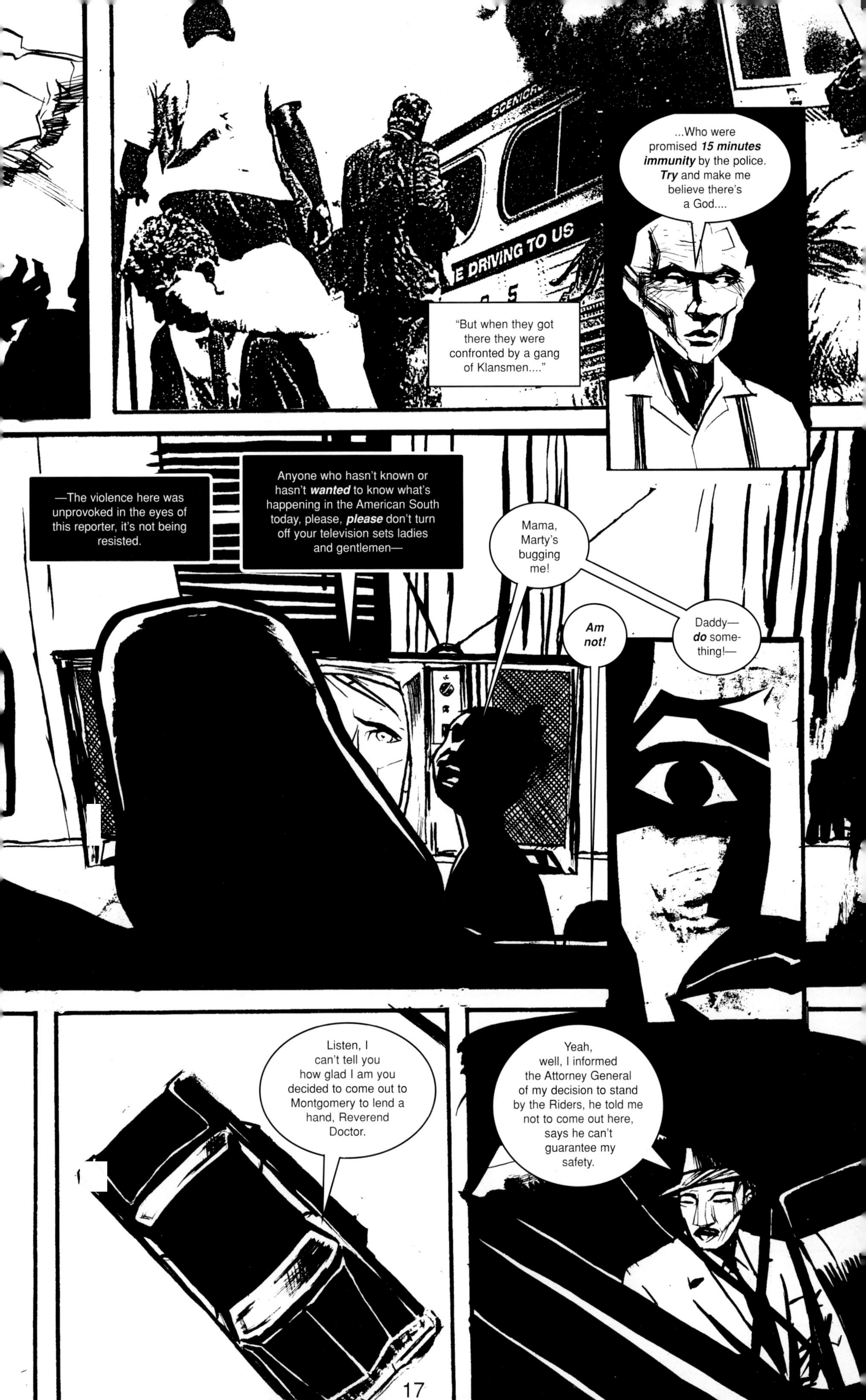

"But when they got there they were confronted by a gang of Klansmen...."
...Who were promised ***15 minutes immunity*** by the police. ***Try*** and make me believe there's a God....
—The violence here was unprovoked in the eyes of this reporter, it's not being resisted.
Anyone who hasn't known or hasn't ***wanted*** to know what's happening in the American South today, please, ***please*** don't turn off your television sets ladies and gentlemen—
Mama, Marty's bugging me!
Am not!
Daddy— ***do*** some-thing!—
Listen, I can't tell you how glad I am you decided to come out to Montgomery to lend a hand, Reverend Doctor.
Yeah, well, I informed the Attorney General of my decision to stand by the Riders, he told me not to come out here, says he can't guarantee my safety.

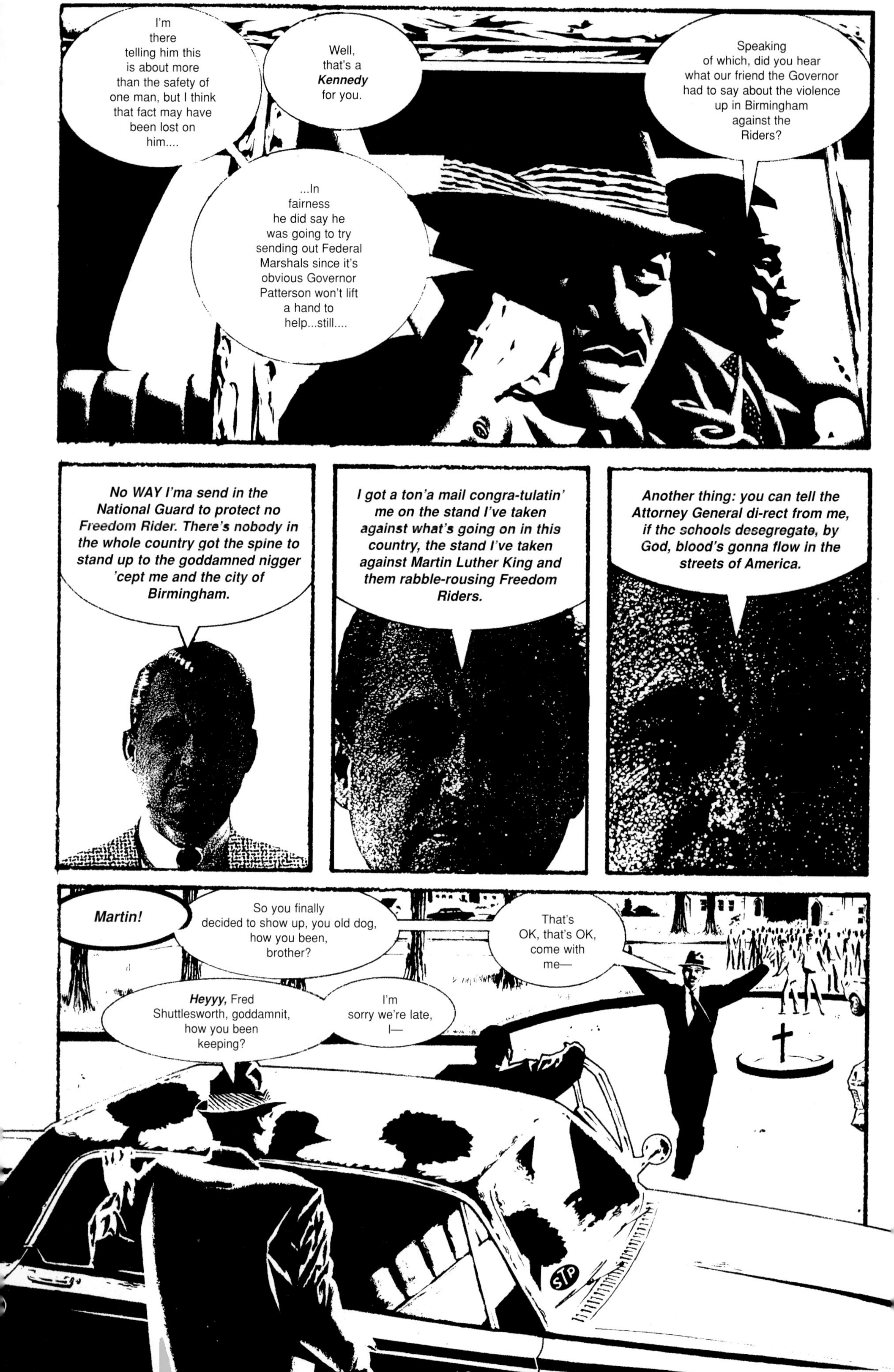

I'm there telling him this is about more than the safety of one man, but I think that fact may have been lost on him....
Well, that's a ***Kennedy*** for you.
...In fairness he did say he was going to try sending out Federal Marshals since it's obvious Governor Patterson won't lift a hand to help...still....
Speaking of which, did you hear what our friend the Governor had to say about the violence up in Birmingham against the Riders?
No WAY I'ma send in the National Guard to protect no Freedom Rider. There's nobody in the whole country got the spine to stand up to the goddamned nigger 'cept me and the city of Birmingham.
I got a ton'a mail congra-tulatin' me on the stand I've taken against what's going on in this country, the stand I've taken against Martin Luther King and them rabble-rousing Freedom Riders.
Another thing: you can tell the Attorney General di-rect from me, if the schools desegregate, by God, blood's gonna flow in the streets of America.
Martin!
So you finally decided to show up, you old dog, how you been, brother?
That's OK, that's OK, come with me—
Heyyy, Fred Shuttlesworth, goddamnit, how you been keeping?
I'm sorry we're late, I—

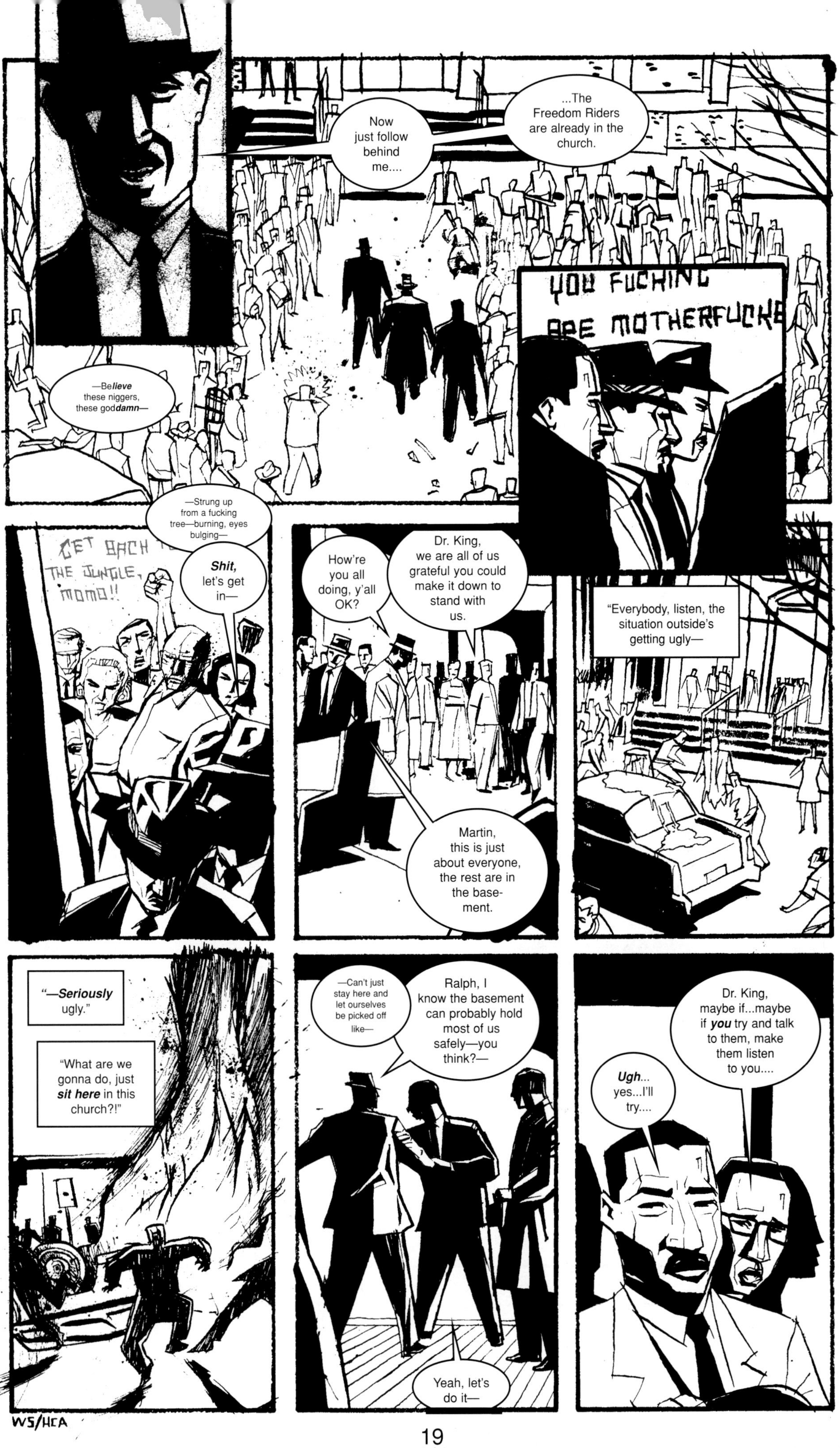
Now just follow behind me....
...The Freedom Riders are already in the church.
YOU FUCKING
ARE MOTHERFUCK
—Believe these niggers, these goddamn—
—Strung up from a fucking tree—burning, eyes bulging—
THE JUNGLE, MOMO!!
Shit, let's get in—
How're you all doing, y'all OK?
Dr. King, we are all of us grateful you could make it down to stand with us.
Martin, this is just about everyone, the rest are in the base-ment.
"Everybody, listen, the situation outside's getting ugly—
"—Seriously ugly."
"What are we gonna do, just sit here in this church?!"
—Can't just stay here and let ourselves be picked off like—
Ralph, I know the basement can probably hold most of us safely—you think?—
Yeah, let's do it—
Dr. King, maybe if...maybe if you try and talk to them, make them listen to you....
Ugh... yes...I'll try....
WS/HCA

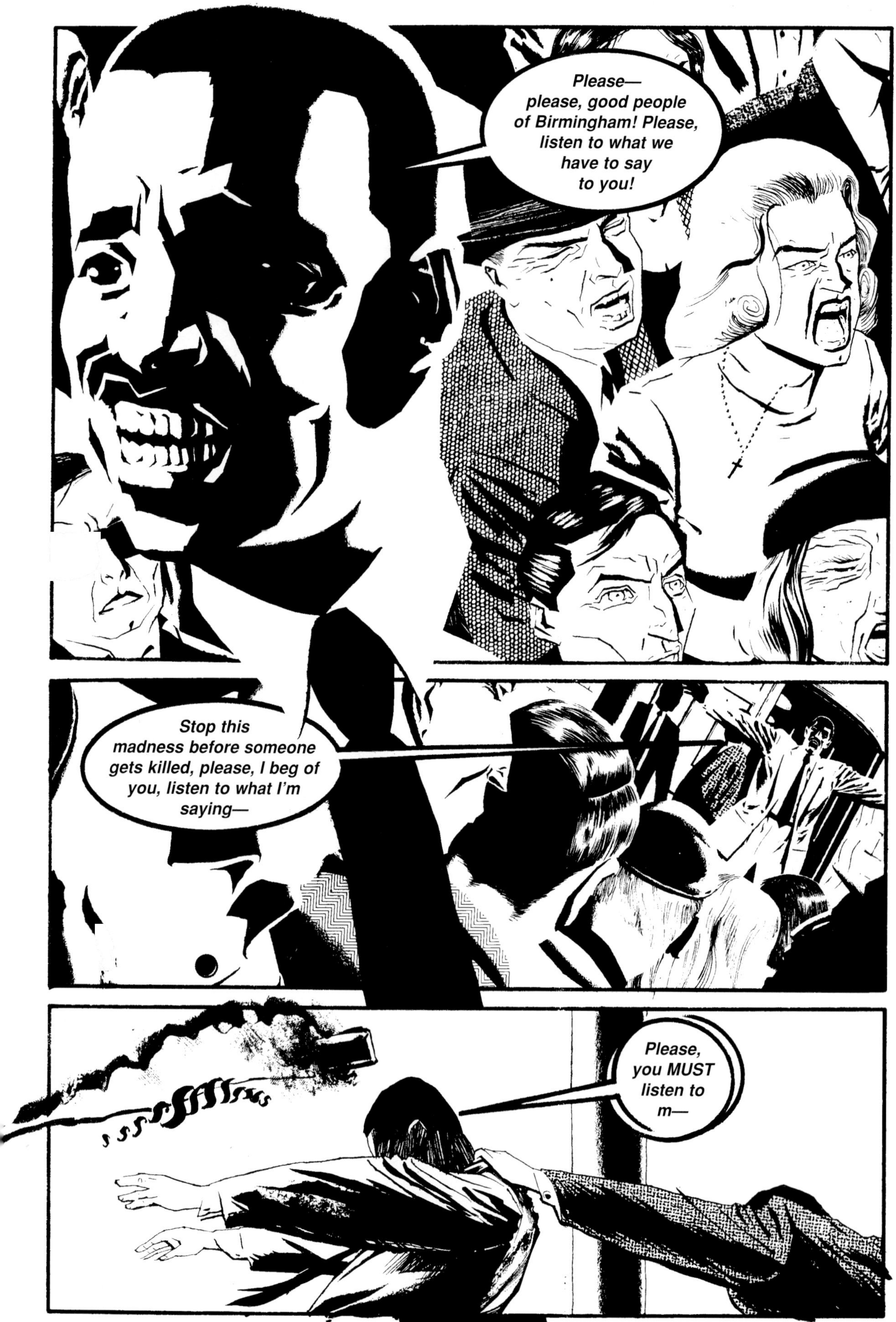
Please—please, good people of Birmingham! Please, listen to what we have to say to you!
Stop this madness before someone gets killed, please, I beg of you, listen to what I'm saying—
Please, you MUST listen to m—

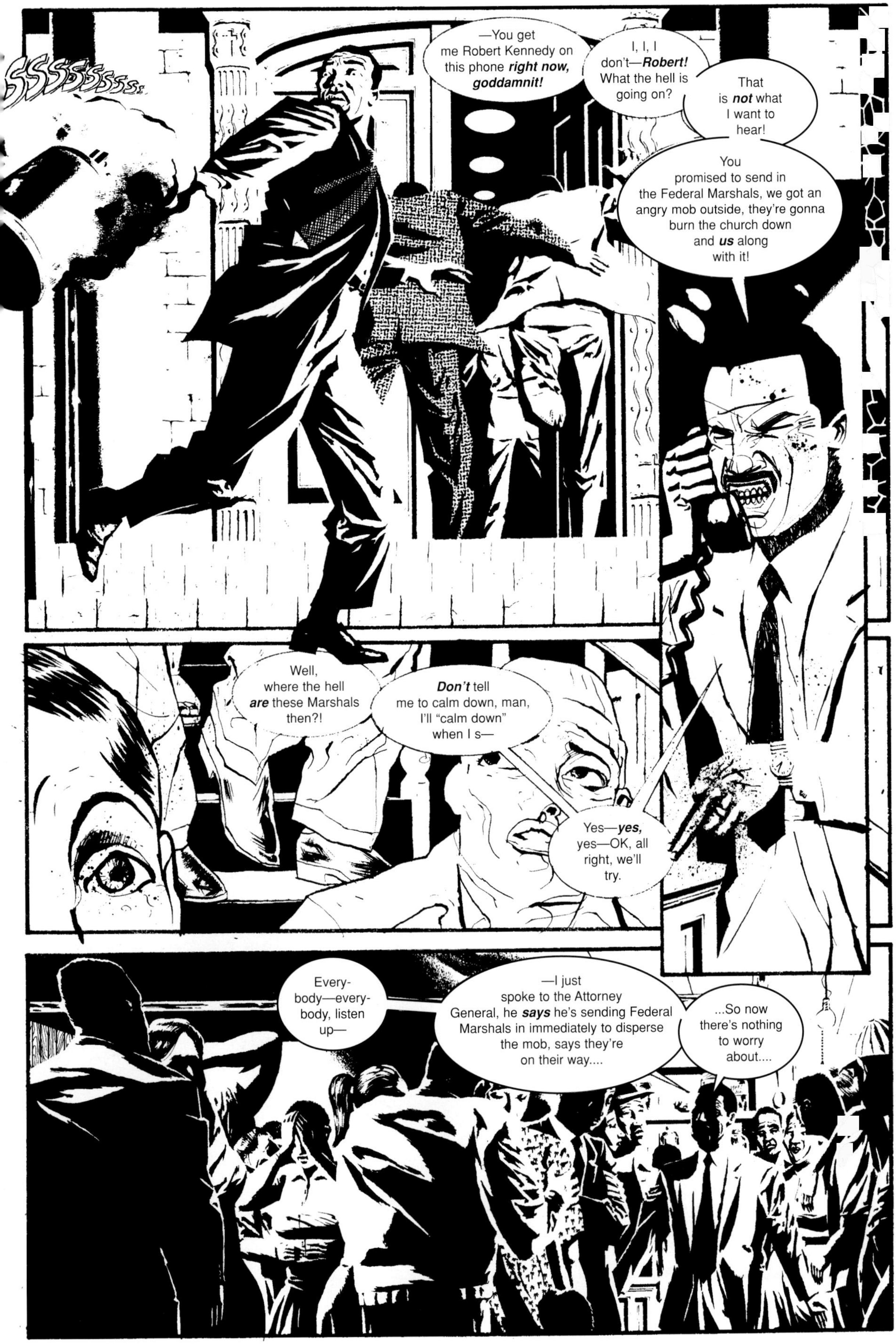
SSSSSSSSss
—You get me Robert Kennedy on this phone **right now, goddamnit!**
I, I, I don't—**Robert!** What the hell is going on?
That is **not** what I want to hear!
You promised to send in the Federal Marshals, we got an angry mob outside, they're gonna burn the church down and **us** along with it!
Well, where the hell **are** these Marshals then?!
Don't tell me to calm down, man, I'll "calm down" when I s—
Yes—***yes,*** yes—OK, all right, we'll try.
Every-body—every-body, listen up—
—I just spoke to the Attorney General, he **says** he's sending Federal Marshals in immediately to disperse the mob, says they're on their way....
...So now there's nothing to worry about....

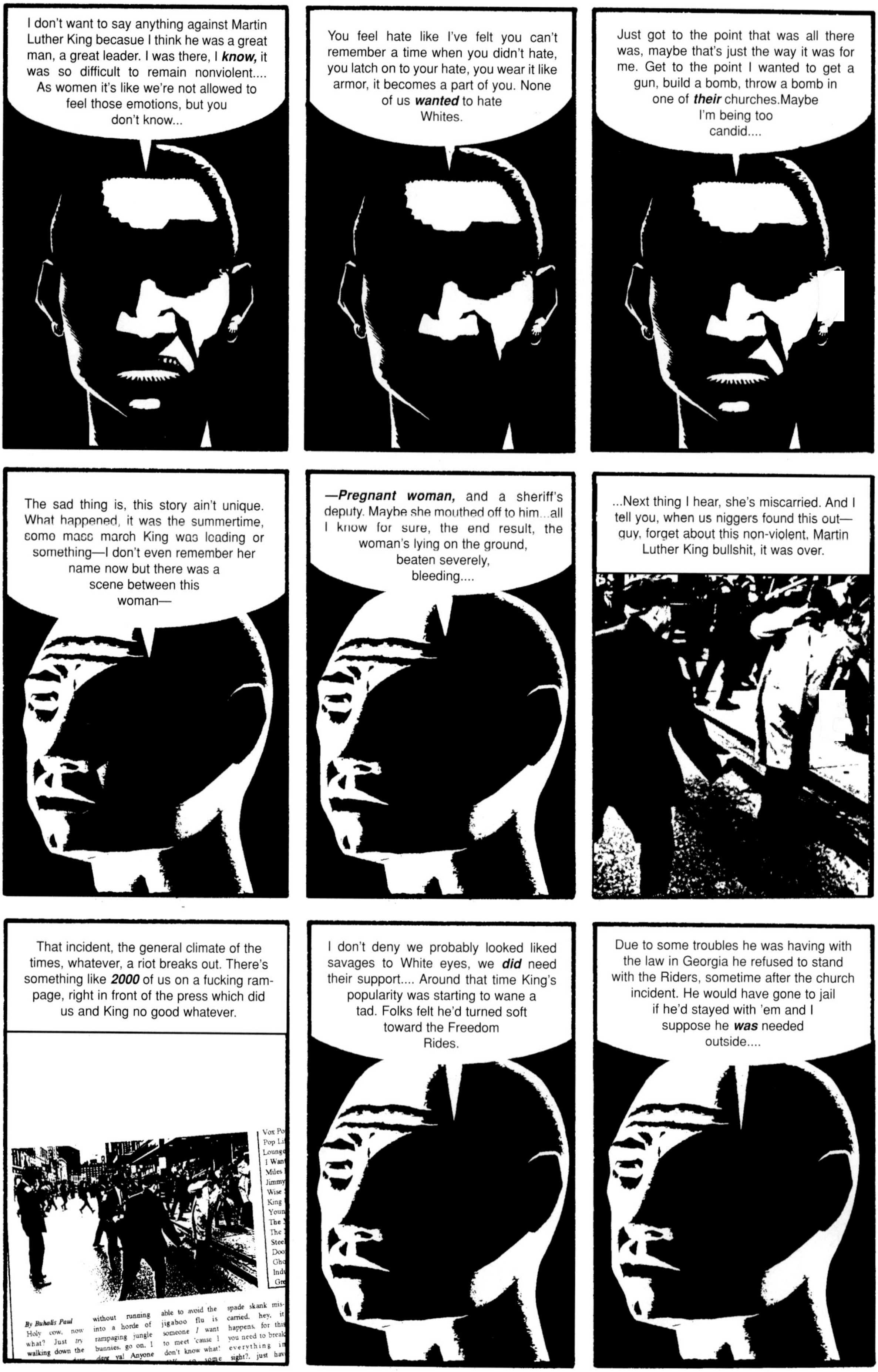
I don't want to say anything against Martin Luther King becasue I think he was a great man, a great leader. I was there, I ***know,*** it was so difficult to remain nonviolent.... As women it's like we're not allowed to feel those emotions, but you don't know...
You feel hate like I've felt you can't remember a time when you didn't hate, you latch on to your hate, you wear it like armor, it becomes a part of you. None of us ***wanted*** to hate Whites.
Just got to the point that was all there was, maybe that's just the way it was for me. Get to the point I wanted to get a gun, build a bomb, throw a bomb in one of ***their*** churches.Maybe I'm being too candid....
The sad thing is, this story ain't unique. What happened, it was the summertime, some mass march King was leading or something—I don't even remember her name now but there was a scene between this woman—
—***Pregnant woman,*** and a sheriff's deputy. Maybe she mouthed off to him...all I know for sure, the end result, the woman's lying on the ground, beaten severely, bleeding....
...Next thing I hear, she's miscarried. And I tell you, when us niggers found this out—guy, forget about this non-violent, Martin Luther King bullshit, it was over.
That incident, the general climate of the times, whatever, a riot breaks out. There's something like ***2000*** of us on a fucking rampage, right in front of the press which did us and King no good whatever.
I don't deny we probably looked liked savages to White eyes, we ***did*** need their support.... Around that time King's popularity was starting to wane a tad. Folks felt he'd turned soft toward the Freedom Rides.
Due to some troubles he was having with the law in Georgia he refused to stand with the Riders, sometime after the church incident. He would have gone to jail if he'd stayed with 'em and I suppose he ***was*** needed outside....

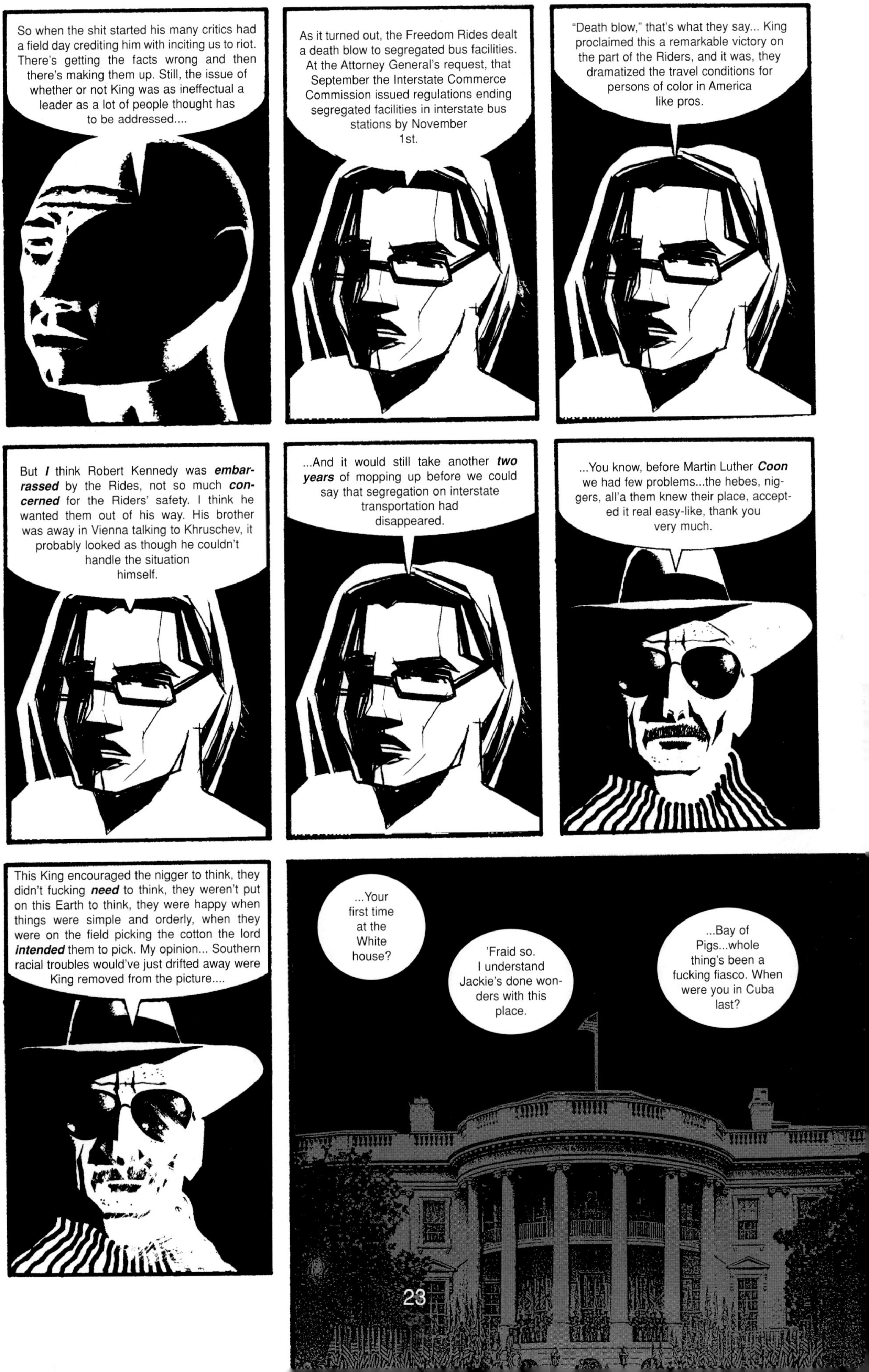
So when the shit started his many critics had a field day crediting him with inciting us to riot. There's getting the facts wrong and then there's making them up. Still, the issue of whether or not King was as ineffectual a leader as a lot of people thought has to be addressed....
As it turned out, the Freedom Rides dealt a death blow to segregated bus facilities. At the Attorney General's request, that September the Interstate Commerce Commission issued regulations ending segregated facilities in interstate bus stations by November 1st.
"Death blow," that's what they say... King proclaimed this a remarkable victory on the part of the Riders, and it was, they dramatized the travel conditions for persons of color in America like pros.
But *I* think Robert Kennedy was ***embarrassed*** by the Rides, not so much ***concerned*** for the Riders' safety. I think he wanted them out of his way. His brother was away in Vienna talking to Khruschev, it probably looked as though he couldn't handle the situation himself.
...And it would still take another ***two years*** of mopping up before we could say that segregation on interstate transportation had disappeared.
...You know, before Martin Luther ***Coon*** we had few problems...the hebes, niggers, all'a them knew their place, accepted it real easy-like, thank you very much.
This King encouraged the nigger to think, they didn't fucking ***need*** to think, they weren't put on this Earth to think, they were happy when things were simple and orderly, when they were on the field picking the cotton the lord ***intended*** them to pick. My opinion... Southern racial troubles would've just drifted away were King removed from the picture....
...Your first time at the White house?
'Fraid so. I understand Jackie's done wonders with this place.
...Bay of Pigs...whole thing's been a fucking fiasco. When were you in Cuba last?

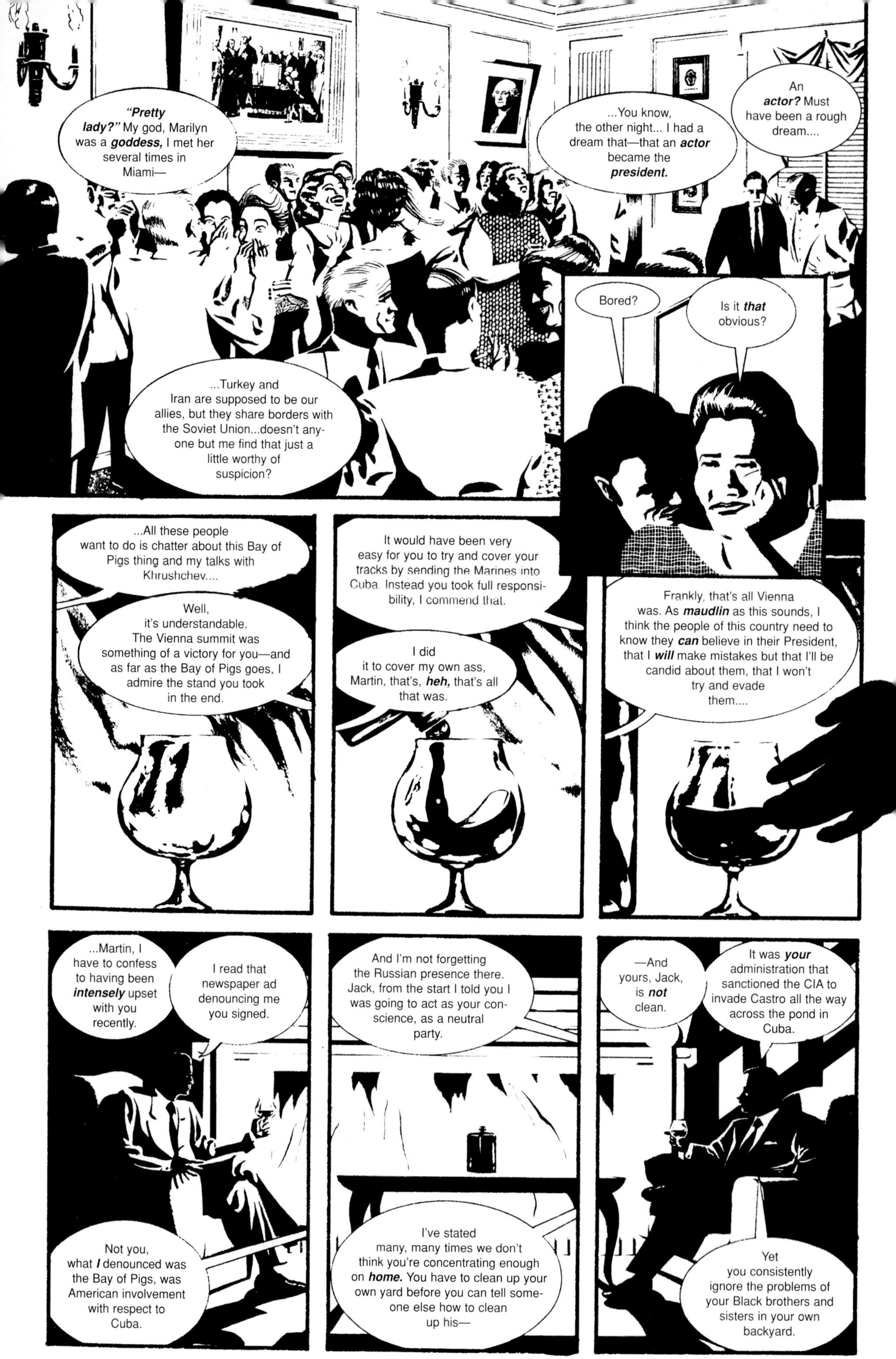
"Pretty lady?" My god, Marilyn was a goddess, I met her several times in Miami—
...You know, the other night... I had a dream that—that an actor became the president.
An actor? Must have been a rough dream....
...Turkey and Iran are supposed to be our allies, but they share borders with the Soviet Union...doesn't anyone but me find that just a little worthy of suspicion?
Bored?
Is it that obvious?
...All these people want to do is chatter about this Bay of Pigs thing and my talks with Khrushchev....
Well, it's understandable. The Vienna summit was something of a victory for you—and as far as the Bay of Pigs goes, I admire the stand you took in the end.
It would have been very easy for you to try and cover your tracks by sending the Marines into Cuba. Instead you took full responsibility, I commend that.
I did it to cover my own ass, Martin, that's, heh, that's all that was.
Frankly, that's all Vienna was. As maudlin as this sounds, I think the people of this country need to know they can believe in their President, that I will make mistakes but that I'll be candid about them, that I won't try and evade them....
...Martin, I have to confess to having been intensely upset with you recently.
I read that newspaper ad denouncing me you signed.
Not you, what I denounced was the Bay of Pigs, was American involvement with respect to Cuba.
And I'm not forgetting the Russian presence there. Jack, from the start I told you I was going to act as your conscience, as a neutral party.
I've stated many, many times we don't think you're concentrating enough on home. You have to clean up your own yard before you can tell someone else how to clean up his—
—And yours, Jack, is not clean.
It was your administration that sanctioned the CIA to invade Castro all the way across the pond in Cuba.
Yet you consistently ignore the problems of your Black brothers and sisters in your own backyard.

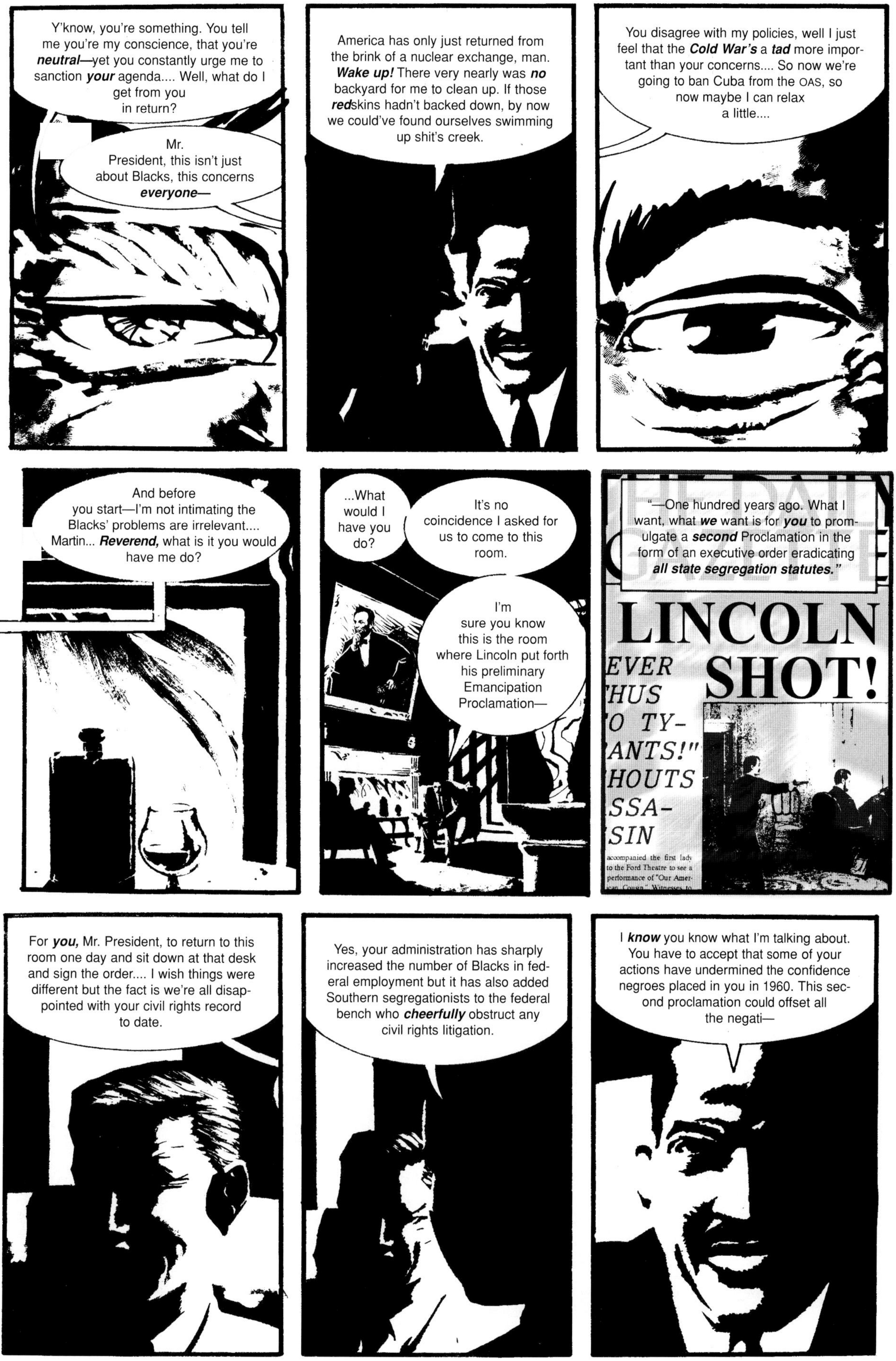
Y'know, you're something. You tell me you're my conscience, that you're *neutral*—yet you constantly urge me to sanction *your* agenda.... Well, what do I get from you in return?
Mr. President, this isn't just about Blacks, this concerns *everyone*—
America has only just returned from the brink of a nuclear exchange, man. *Wake up!* There very nearly was *no* backyard for me to clean up. If those *red*skins hadn't backed down, by now we could've found ourselves swimming up shit's creek.
You disagree with my policies, well I just feel that the *Cold War's* a *tad* more important than your concerns.... So now we're going to ban Cuba from the OAS, so now maybe I can relax a little....
And before you start—I'm not intimating the Blacks' problems are irrelevant.... Martin... *Reverend,* what is it you would have me do?
...What would I have you do?
It's no coincidence I asked for us to come to this room.
I'm sure you know this is the room where Lincoln put forth his preliminary Emancipation Proclamation—
"—One hundred years ago. What I want, what *we* want is for *you* to promulgate a *second* Proclamation in the form of an executive order eradicating *all state segregation statutes.*"
LINCOLN SHOT!
accompanied the first lady to the Ford Theatre to see a performance of "Our Amer-
For *you,* Mr. President, to return to this room one day and sit down at that desk and sign the order.... I wish things were different but the fact is we're all disappointed with your civil rights record to date.
Yes, your administration has sharply increased the number of Blacks in federal employment but it has also added Southern segregationists to the federal bench who *cheerfully* obstruct any civil rights litigation.
I *know* you know what I'm talking about. You have to accept that some of your actions have undermined the confidence negroes placed in you in 1960. This second proclamation could offset all the negati—

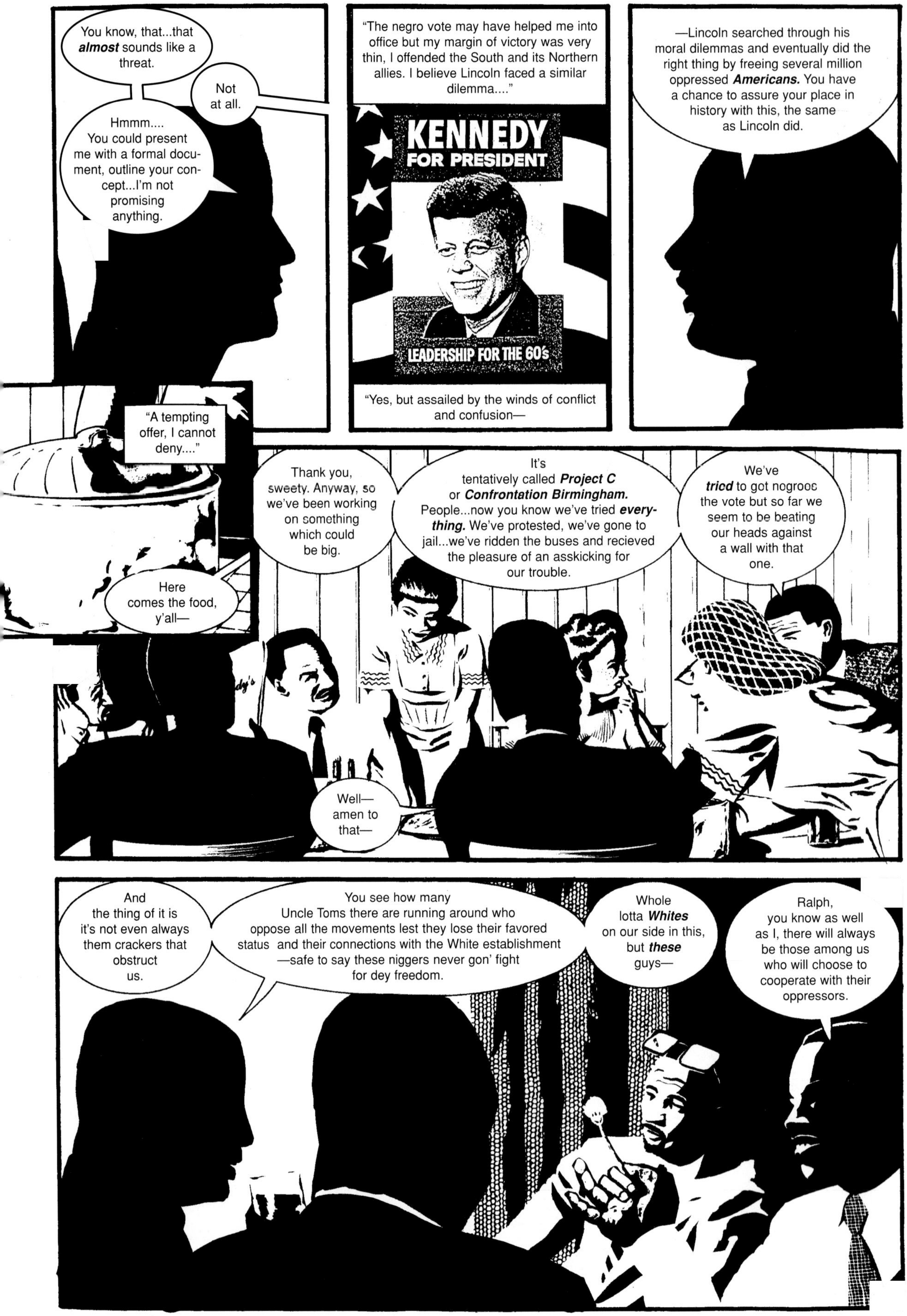
You know, that...that *almost* sounds like a threat.
Not at all.
Hmmm.... You could present me with a formal document, outline your concept...I'm not promising anything.
"The negro vote may have helped me into office but my margin of victory was very thin, I offended the South and its Northern allies. I believe Lincoln faced a similar dilemma...."
KENNEDY
FOR PRESIDENT
LEADERSHIP FOR THE 60's
"Yes, but assailed by the winds of conflict and confusion—
—Lincoln searched through his moral dilemmas and eventually did the right thing by freeing several million oppressed *Americans.* You have a chance to assure your place in history with this, the same as Lincoln did.
"A tempting offer, I cannot deny...."
Here comes the food, y'all—
Thank you, sweety. Anyway, so we've been working on something which could be big.
It's tentatively called *Project C* or *Confrontation Birmingham.* People...now you know we've tried *everything.* We've protested, we've gone to jail...we've ridden the buses and recieved the pleasure of an asskicking for our trouble.
We've *tried* to get negroes the vote but so far we seem to be beating our heads against a wall with that one.
Well— amen to that—
And the thing of it is it's not even always them crackers that obstruct us.
You see how many Uncle Toms there are running around who oppose all the movements lest they lose their favored status and their connections with the White establishment —safe to say these niggers never gon' fight for dey freedom.
Whole lotta *Whites* on our side in this, but *these* guys—
Ralph, you know as well as I, there will always be those among us who will choose to cooperate with their oppressors.

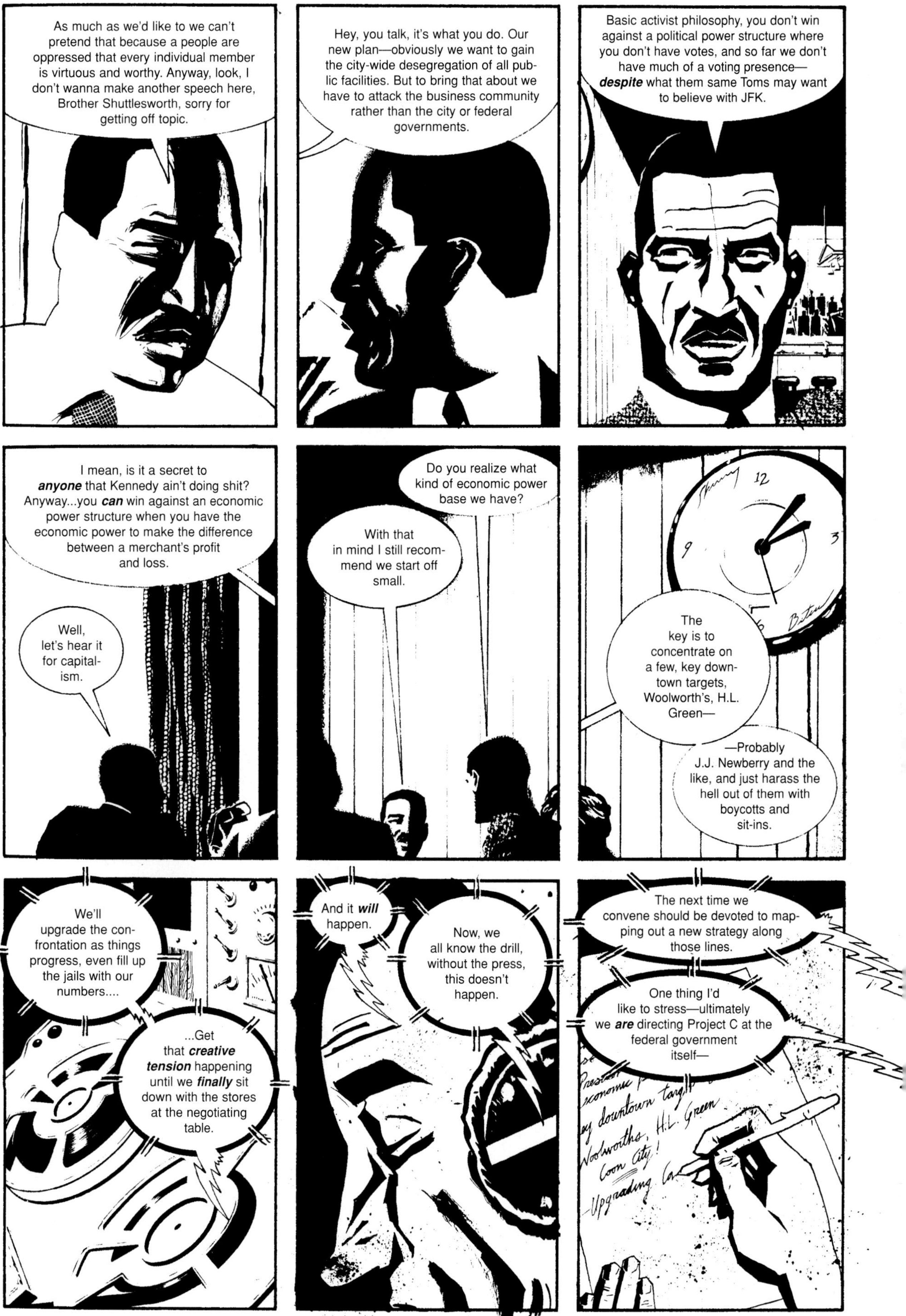
As much as we'd like to we can't pretend that because a people are oppressed that every individual member is virtuous and worthy. Anyway, look, I don't wanna make another speech here, Brother Shuttlesworth, sorry for getting off topic.
Hey, you talk, it's what you do. Our new plan—obviously we want to gain the city-wide desegregation of all public facilities. But to bring that about we have to attack the business community rather than the city or federal governments.
Basic activist philosophy, you don't win against a political power structure where you don't have votes, and so far we don't have much of a voting presence—**despite** what them same Toms may want to believe with JFK.
I mean, is it a secret to **anyone** that Kennedy ain't doing shit? Anyway...you **can** win against an economic power structure when you have the economic power to make the difference between a merchant's profit and loss.
Well, let's hear it for capitalism.
Do you realize what kind of economic power base we have?
With that in mind I still recommend we start off small.
The key is to concentrate on a few, key downtown targets, Woolworth's, H.L. Green—
—Probably J.J. Newberry and the like, and just harass the hell out of them with boycotts and sit-ins.
We'll upgrade the confrontation as things progress, even fill up the jails with our numbers....
...Get that **creative tension** happening until we **finally** sit down with the stores at the negotiating table.
And it **will** happen.
Now, we all know the drill, without the press, this doesn't happen.
The next time we convene should be devoted to mapping out a new strategy along those lines.
One thing I'd like to stress—ultimately we **are** directing Project C at the federal government itself—

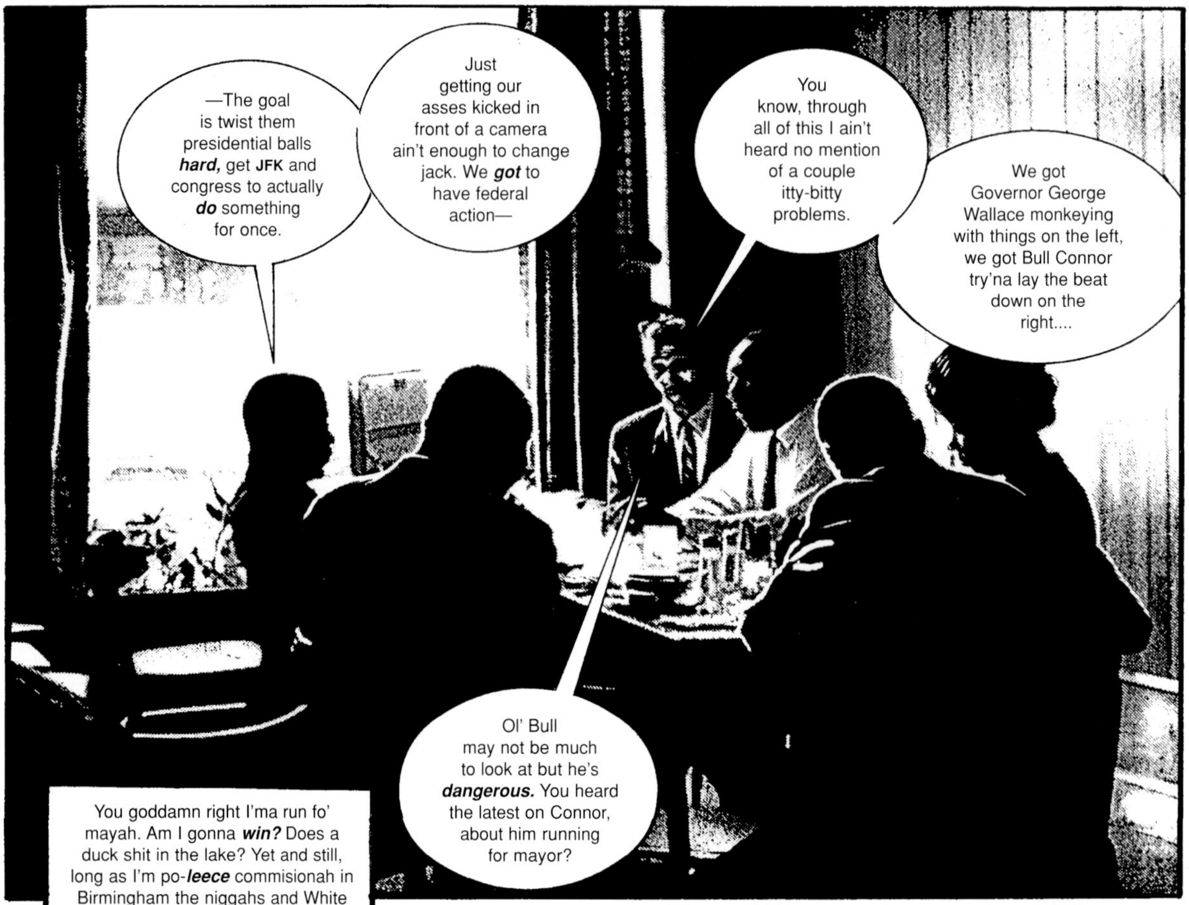
—The goal is twist them presidential balls ***hard,*** get **JFK** and congress to actually ***do*** something for once.
Just getting our asses kicked in front of a camera ain't enough to change jack. We ***got*** to have federal action—
You know, through all of this I ain't heard no mention of a couple itty-bitty problems.
We got Governor George Wallace monkeying with things on the left, we got Bull Connor try'na lay the beat down on the right....
Ol' Bull may not be much to look at but he's ***dangerous.*** You heard the latest on Connor, about him running for mayor?

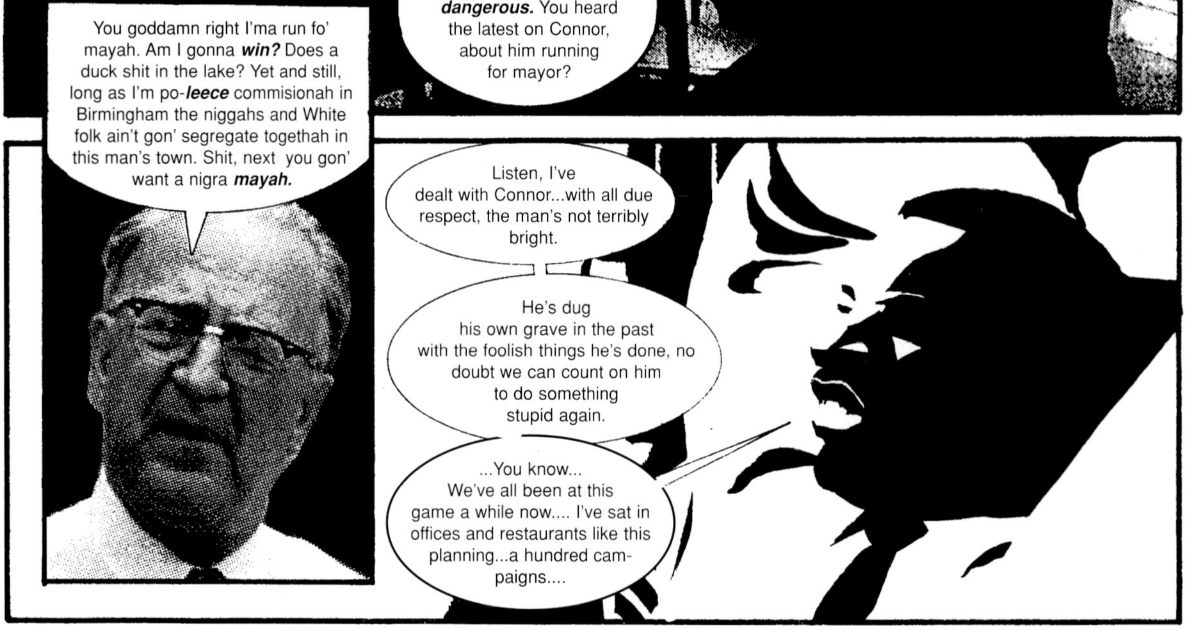
You goddamn right I'ma run fo' mayah. Am I gonna ***win?*** Does a duck shit in the lake? Yet and still, long as I'm po-***leece*** commisionah in Birmingham the niggahs and White folk ain't gon' segregate togethah in this man's town. Shit, next you gon' want a nigra ***mayah.***
Listen, I've dealt with Connor...with all due respect, the man's not terribly bright.
He's dug his own grave in the past with the foolish things he's done, no doubt we can count on him to do something stupid again.
...You know... We've all been at this game a while now.... I've sat in offices and restaurants like this planning...a hundred campaigns....

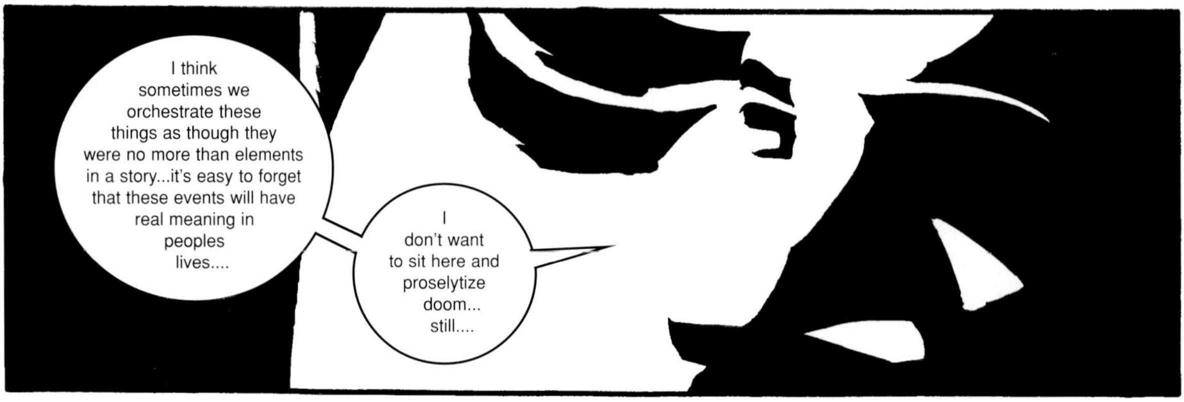
I think sometimes we orchestrate these things as though they were no more than elements in a story...it's easy to forget that these events will have real meaning in peoples lives....
I don't want to sit here and proselytize doom... still....

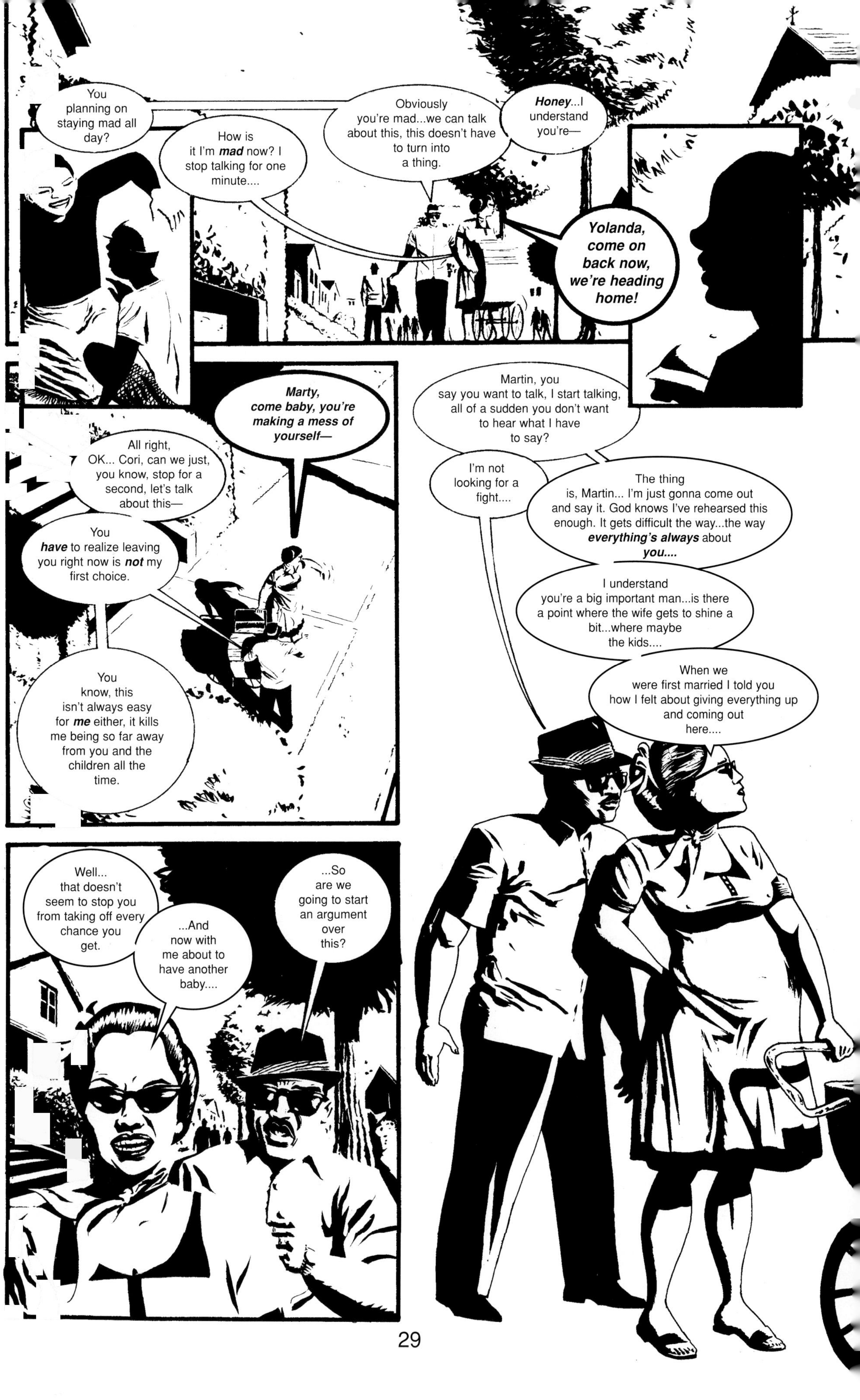
You planning on staying mad all day?
How is it I'm ***mad*** now? I stop talking for one minute....
Obviously you're mad...we can talk about this, this doesn't have to turn into a thing.
Honey...I understand you're—
Yolanda, come on back now, we're heading home!
All right, OK... Cori, can we just, you know, stop for a second, let's talk about this—
Marty, come baby, you're making a mess of yourself—
You ***have*** to realize leaving you right now is ***not*** my first choice.
You know, this isn't always easy for ***me*** either, it kills me being so far away from you and the children all the time.
Martin, you say you want to talk, I start talking, all of a sudden you don't want to hear what I have to say?
I'm not looking for a fight....
The thing is, Martin... I'm just gonna come out and say it. God knows I've rehearsed this enough. It gets difficult the way...the way ***everything's always*** about ***you....***
I understand you're a big important man...is there a point where the wife gets to shine a bit...where maybe the kids....
When we were first married I told you how I felt about giving everything up and coming out here....
Well... that doesn't seem to stop you from taking off every chance you get.
...And now with me about to have another baby....
...So are we going to start an argument over this?

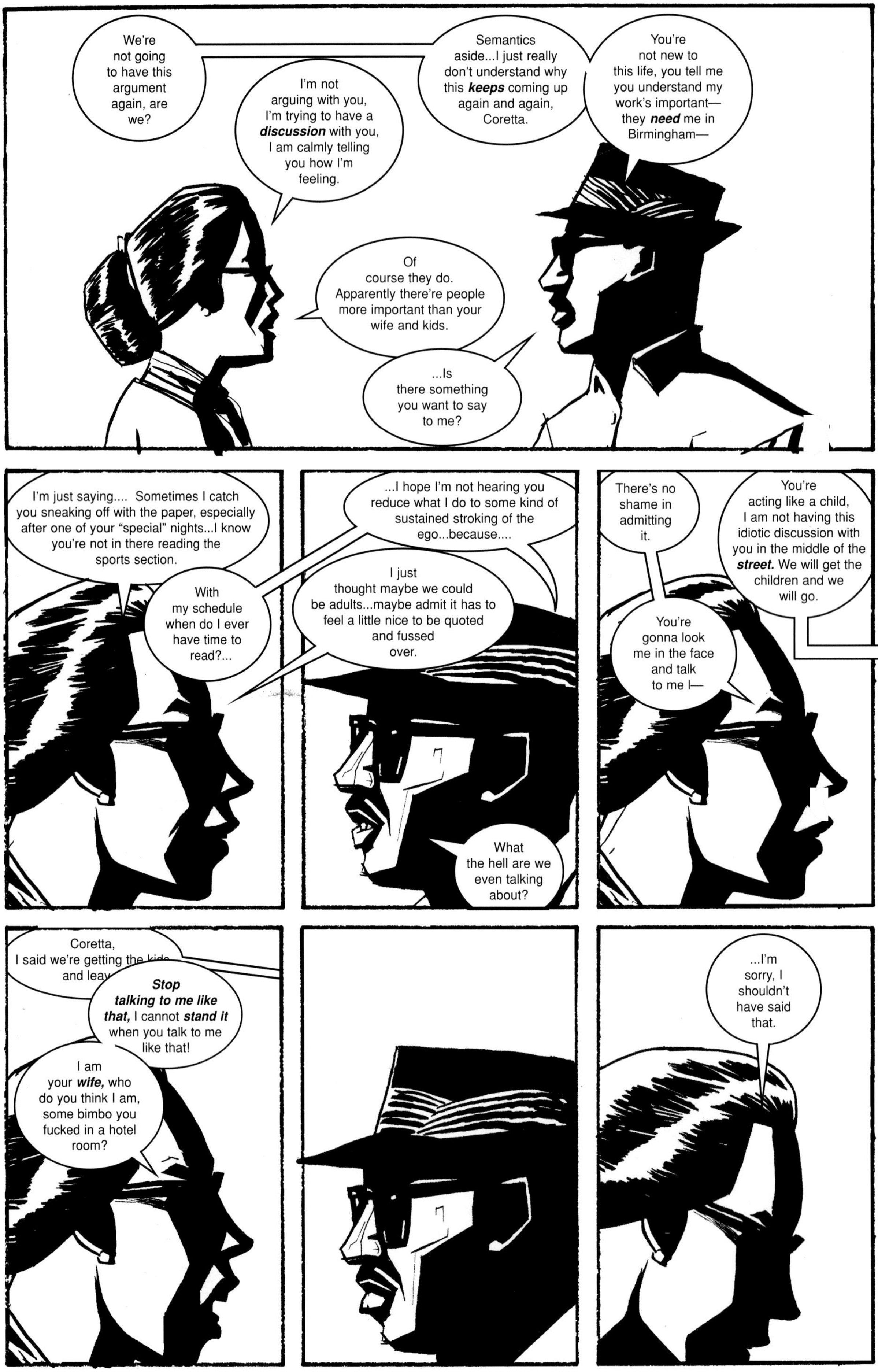
We're not going to have this argument again, are we?
I'm not arguing with you, I'm trying to have a **discussion** with you, I am calmly telling you how I'm feeling.
Semantics aside...I just really don't understand why this **keeps** coming up again and again, Coretta.
You're not new to this life, you tell me you understand my work's important— they **need** me in Birmingham—
Of course they do. Apparently there're people more important than your wife and kids.
...Is there something you want to say to me?
I'm just saying.... Sometimes I catch you sneaking off with the paper, especially after one of your "special" nights...I know you're not in there reading the sports section.
With my schedule when do I ever have time to read?...
...I hope I'm not hearing you reduce what I do to some kind of sustained stroking of the ego...because....
I just thought maybe we could be adults...maybe admit it has to feel a little nice to be quoted and fussed over.
What the hell are we even talking about?
There's no shame in admitting it.
You're acting like a child, I am not having this idiotic discussion with you in the middle of the **street.** We will get the children and we will go.
You're gonna look me in the face and talk to me I—
Coretta, I said we're getting the kids and leav
Stop talking to me like that, I cannot **stand it** when you talk to me like that!
I am your **wife,** who do you think I am, some bimbo you fucked in a hotel room?
...I'm sorry, I shouldn't have said that.

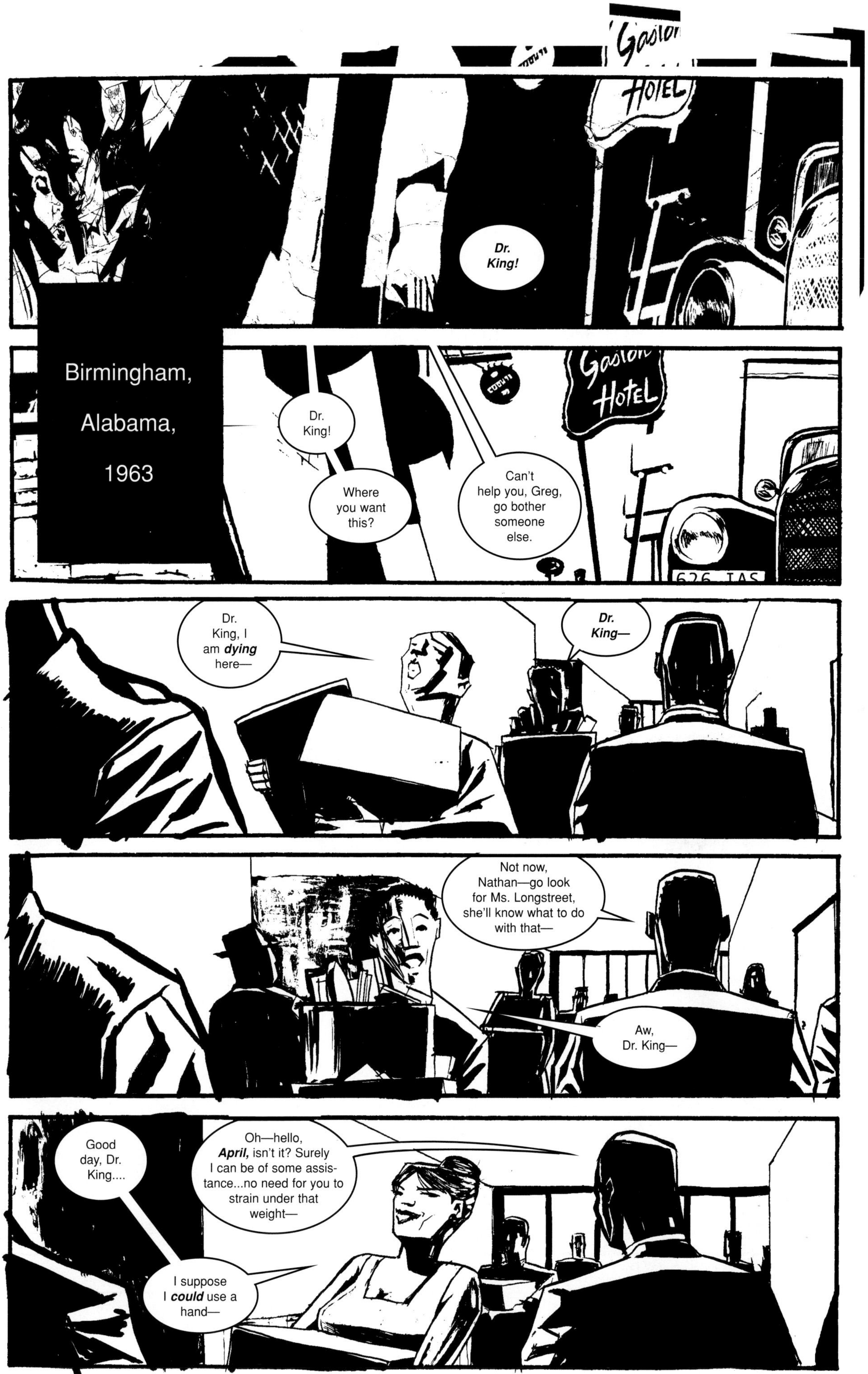

Dr. King!
Birmingham, Alabama, 1963
Dr. King!
Where you want this?
Can't help you, Greg, go bother someone else.
Dr. King, I am *dying* here—
Dr. King—
Not now, Nathan—go look for Ms. Longstreet, she'll know what to do with that—
Aw, Dr. King—
Good day, Dr. King....
Oh—hello, ***April,*** isn't it? Surely I can be of some assistance...no need for you to strain under that weight—
I suppose I ***could*** use a hand—

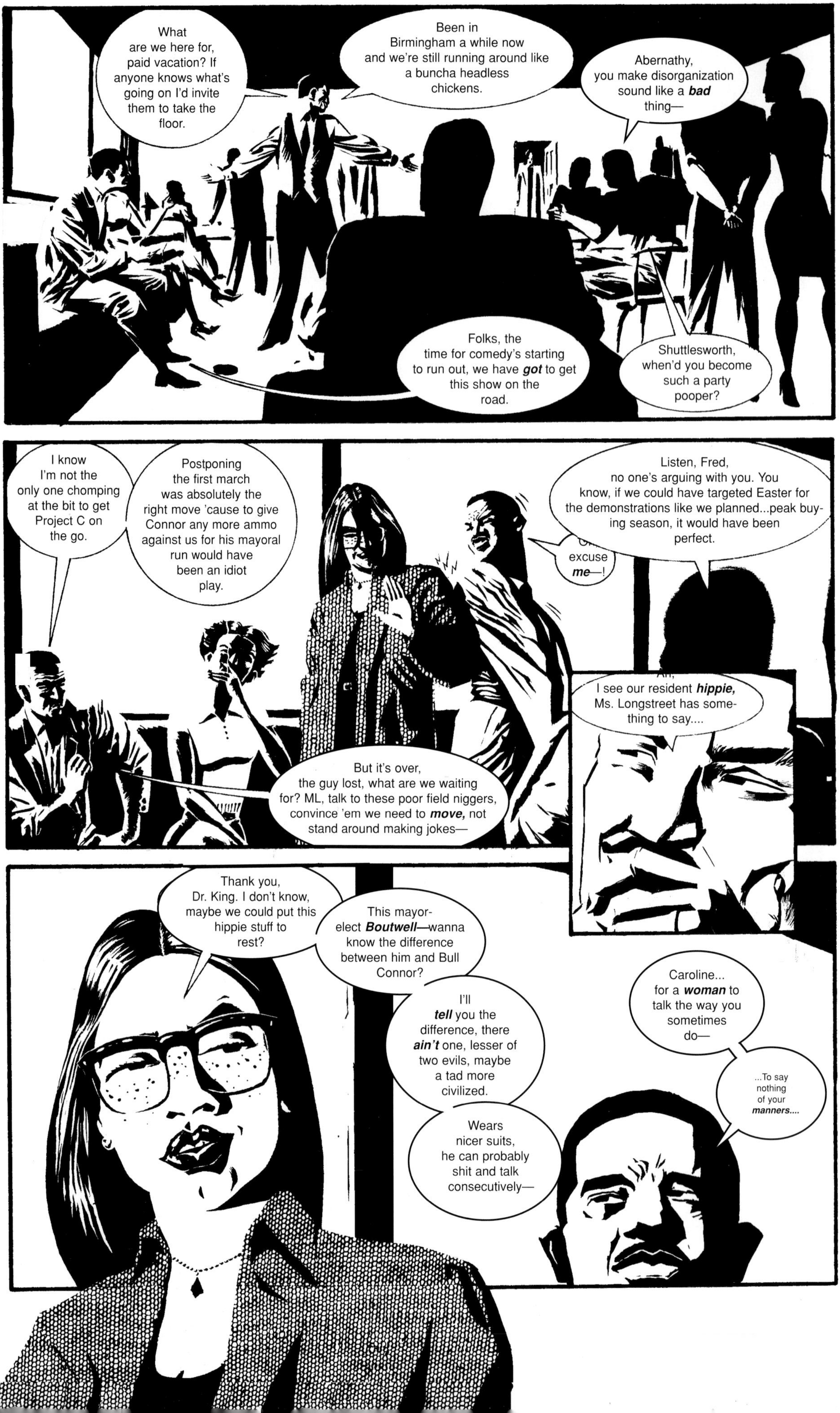
What are we here for, paid vacation? If anyone knows what's going on I'd invite them to take the floor.
Been in Birmingham a while now and we're still running around like a buncha headless chickens.
Abernathy, you make disorganization sound like a ***bad*** thing—
Folks, the time for comedy's starting to run out, we have ***got*** to get this show on the road.
Shuttlesworth, when'd you become such a party pooper?
I know I'm not the only one chomping at the bit to get Project C on the go.
Postponing the first march was absolutely the right move 'cause to give Connor any more ammo against us for his mayoral run would have been an idiot play.
Listen, Fred, no one's arguing with you. You know, if we could have targeted Easter for the demonstrations like we planned...peak buying season, it would have been perfect.
excuse ***me***—!
But it's over, the guy lost, what are we waiting for? ML, talk to these poor field niggers, convince 'em we need to ***move,*** not stand around making jokes—
I see our resident ***hippie,*** Ms. Longstreet has something to say....
Thank you, Dr. King. I don't know, maybe we could put this hippie stuff to rest?
This mayor-elect ***Boutwell***—wanna know the difference between him and Bull Connor?
I'll ***tell*** you the difference, there ***ain't*** one, lesser of two evils, maybe a tad more civilized.
Wears nicer suits, he can probably shit and talk consecutively—
Caroline... for a ***woman*** to talk the way you sometimes do—
...To say nothing of your ***manners....***

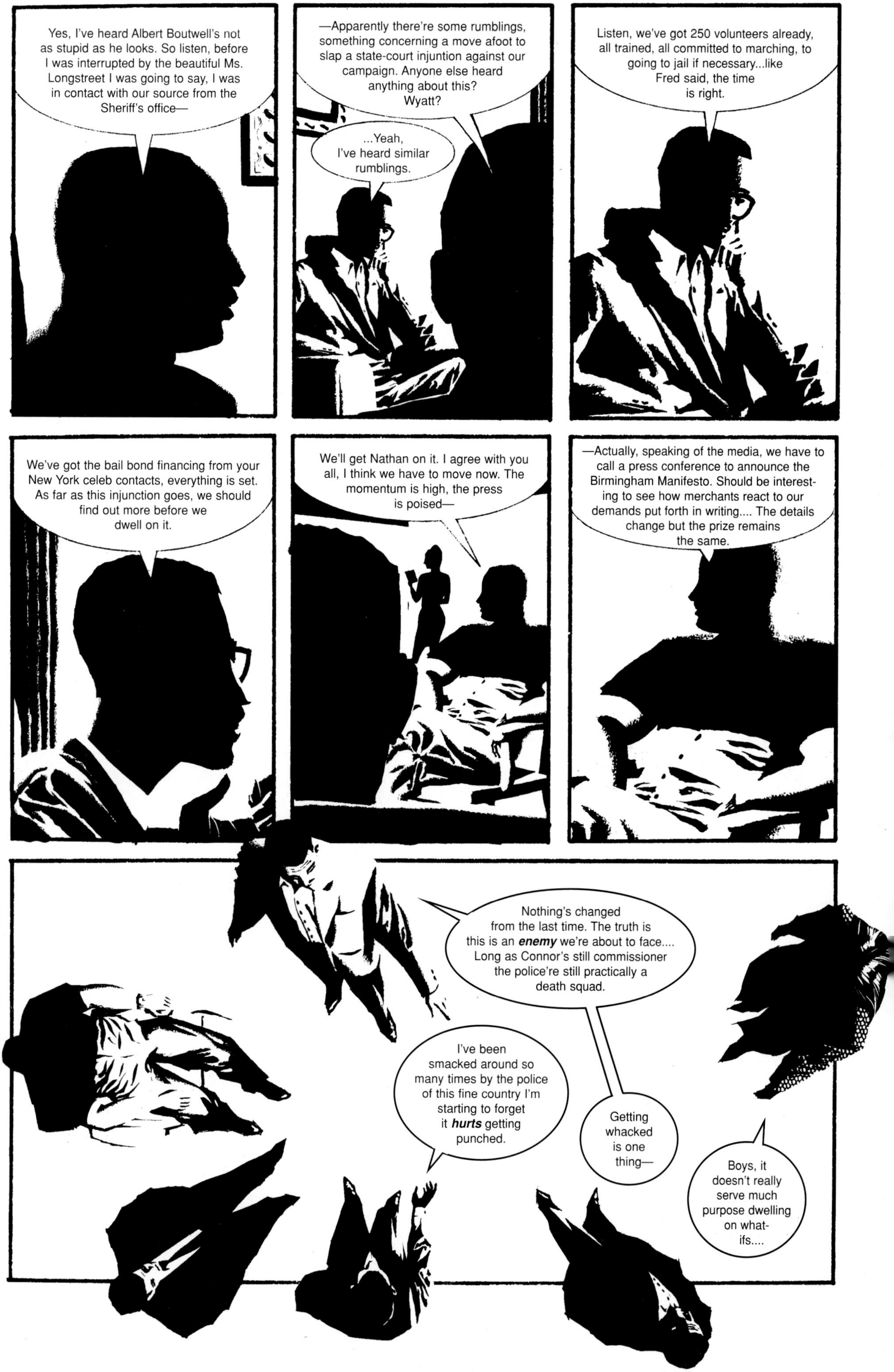
Yes, I've heard Albert Boutwell's not as stupid as he looks. So listen, before I was interrupted by the beautiful Ms. Longstreet I was going to say, I was in contact with our source from the Sheriff's office—
—Apparently there're some rumblings, something concerning a move afoot to slap a state-court injuntion against our campaign. Anyone else heard anything about this? Wyatt?
...Yeah, I've heard similar rumblings.
Listen, we've got 250 volunteers already, all trained, all committed to marching, to going to jail if necessary...like Fred said, the time is right.
We've got the bail bond financing from your New York celeb contacts, everything is set. As far as this injunction goes, we should find out more before we dwell on it.
We'll get Nathan on it. I agree with you all, I think we have to move now. The momentum is high, the press is poised—
—Actually, speaking of the media, we have to call a press conference to announce the Birmingham Manifesto. Should be interesting to see how merchants react to our demands put forth in writing.... The details change but the prize remains the same.
Nothing's changed from the last time. The truth is this is an ***enemy*** we're about to face.... Long as Connor's still commissioner the police're still practically a death squad.
I've been smacked around so many times by the police of this fine country I'm starting to forget it ***hurts*** getting punched.
Getting whacked is one thing—
Boys, it doesn't really serve much purpose dwelling on what-ifs....

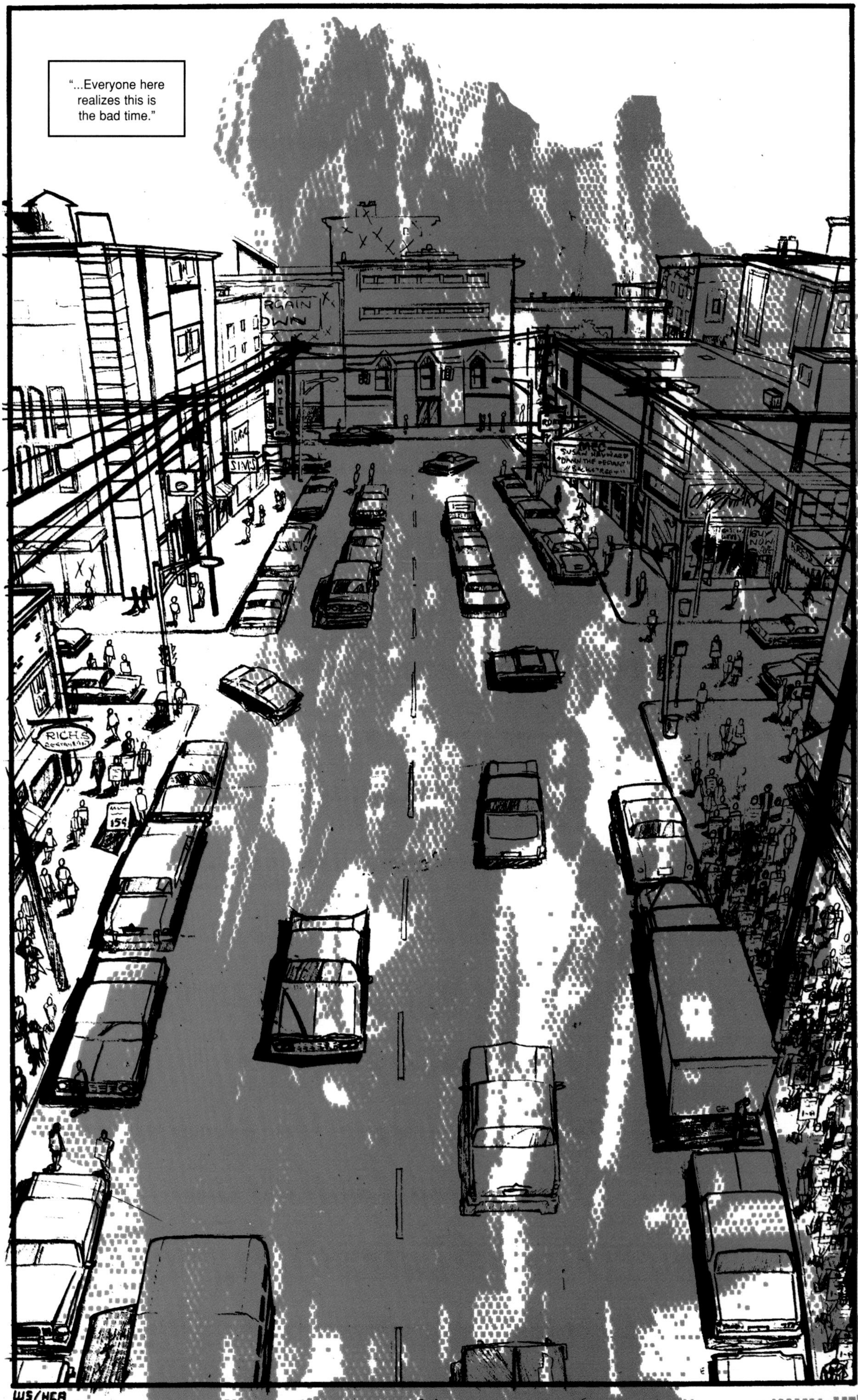
"...Everyone here realizes this is the bad time."
HOTEL
SIMS
RICH'S

WS/HCA

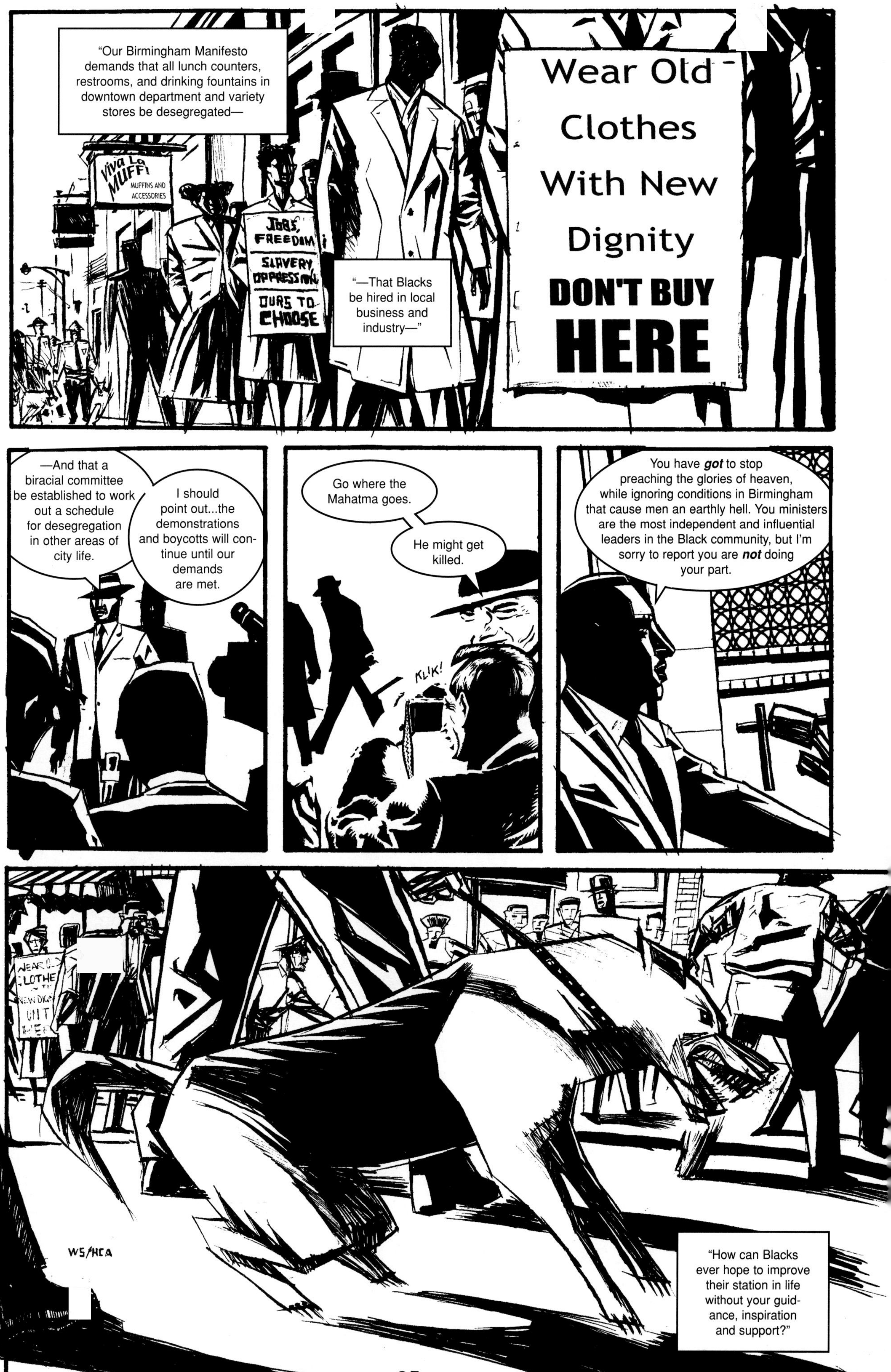
"Our Birmingham Manifesto demands that all lunch counters, restrooms, and drinking fountains in downtown department and variety stores be desegregated—
Viva La MUFFI! MUFFINS AND ACCESSORIES
JOBS, FREEDOM
SLAVERY, OPPRESSION
OURS TO CHOOSE
"—That Blacks be hired in local business and industry—"
Wear Old Clothes With New Dignity
DON'T BUY HERE
—And that a biracial committee be established to work out a schedule for desegregation in other areas of city life.
I should point out...the demonstrations and boycotts will continue until our demands are met.
Go where the Mahatma goes.
He might get killed.
KLIK!
You have ***got*** to stop preaching the glories of heaven, while ignoring conditions in Birmingham that cause men an earthly hell. You ministers are the most independent and influential leaders in the Black community, but I'm sorry to report you are ***not*** doing your part.
WS/HCA
"How can Blacks ever hope to improve their station in life without your guidance, inspiration and support?"

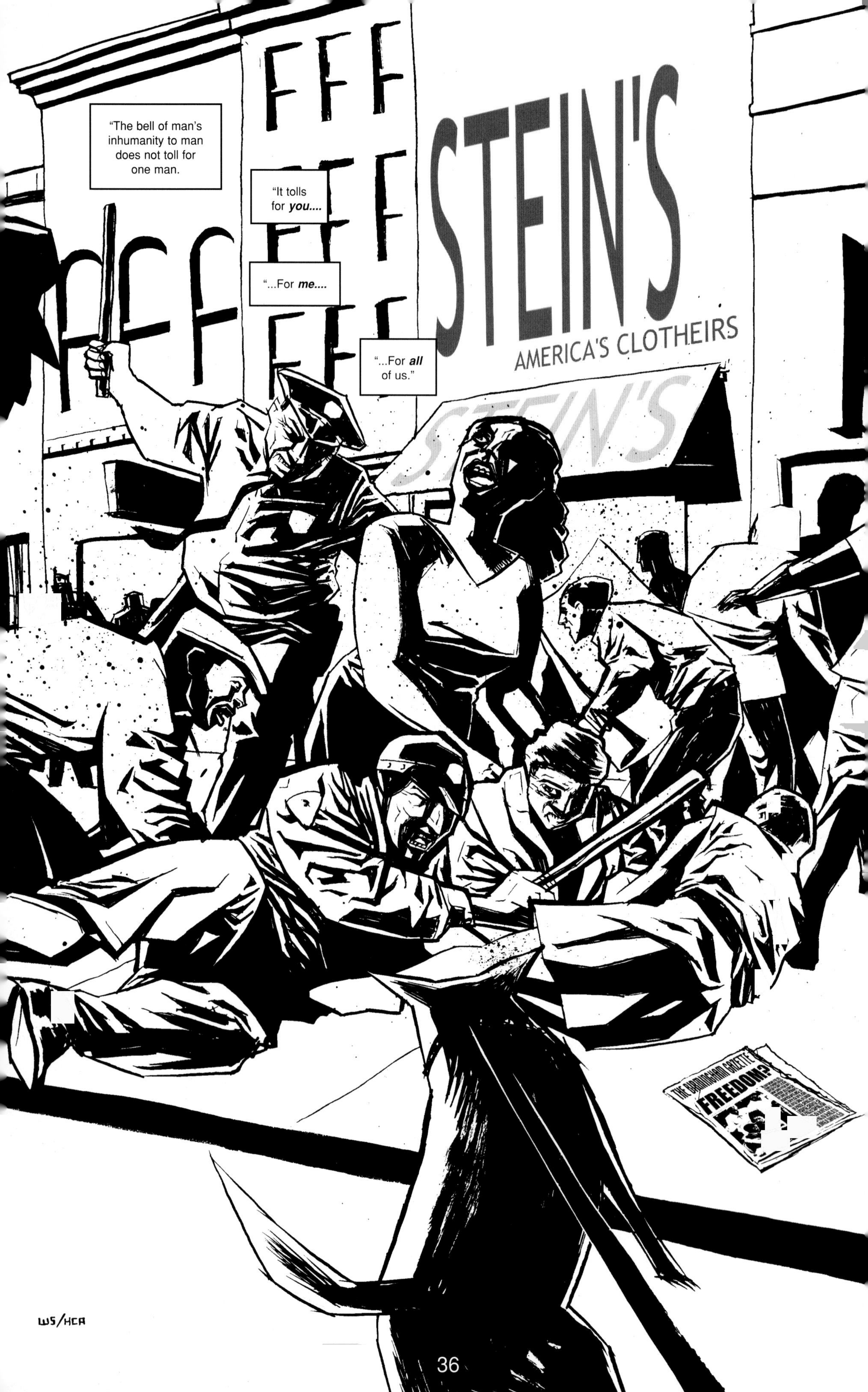

"The bell of man's inhumanity to man does not toll for one man.
"It tolls for ***you....***
"...For ***me....***
"...For ***all*** of us."
STEIN'S
AMERICA'S CLOTHEIRS
STEIN'S
THE BIRMINGHAM GAZETTE
FREEDOM?
WS/HCA

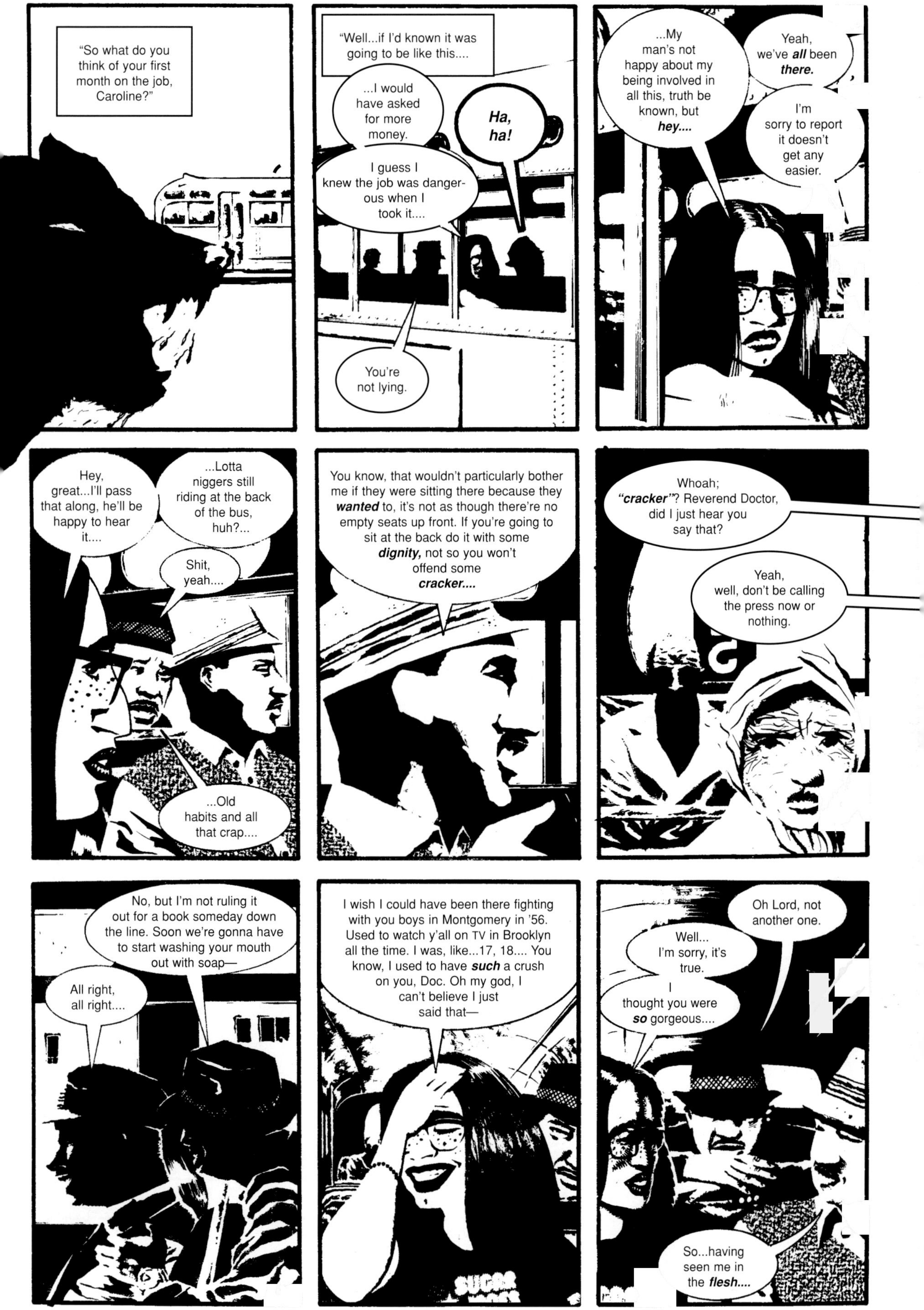
"So what do you think of your first month on the job, Caroline?"
"Well...if I'd known it was going to be like this....
...I would have asked for more money.
Ha, ha!
I guess I knew the job was dangerous when I took it....
You're not lying.
...My man's not happy about my being involved in all this, truth be known, but hey....
Yeah, we've all been there.
I'm sorry to report it doesn't get any easier.
Hey, great...I'll pass that along, he'll be happy to hear it....
...Lotta niggers still riding at the back of the bus, huh?...
Shit, yeah....
...Old habits and all that crap....
You know, that wouldn't particularly bother me if they were sitting there because they wanted to, it's not as though there're no empty seats up front. If you're going to sit at the back do it with some dignity, not so you won't offend some cracker....
Whoah; "cracker"? Reverend Doctor, did I just hear you say that?
Yeah, well, don't be calling the press now or nothing.
No, but I'm not ruling it out for a book someday down the line. Soon we're gonna have to start washing your mouth out with soap—
All right, all right....
I wish I could have been there fighting with you boys in Montgomery in '56. Used to watch y'all on TV in Brooklyn all the time. I was, like...17, 18.... You know, I used to have such a crush on you, Doc. Oh my god, I can't believe I just said that—
Oh Lord, not another one.
Well... I'm sorry, it's true.
I thought you were so gorgeous....
So...having seen me in the flesh....

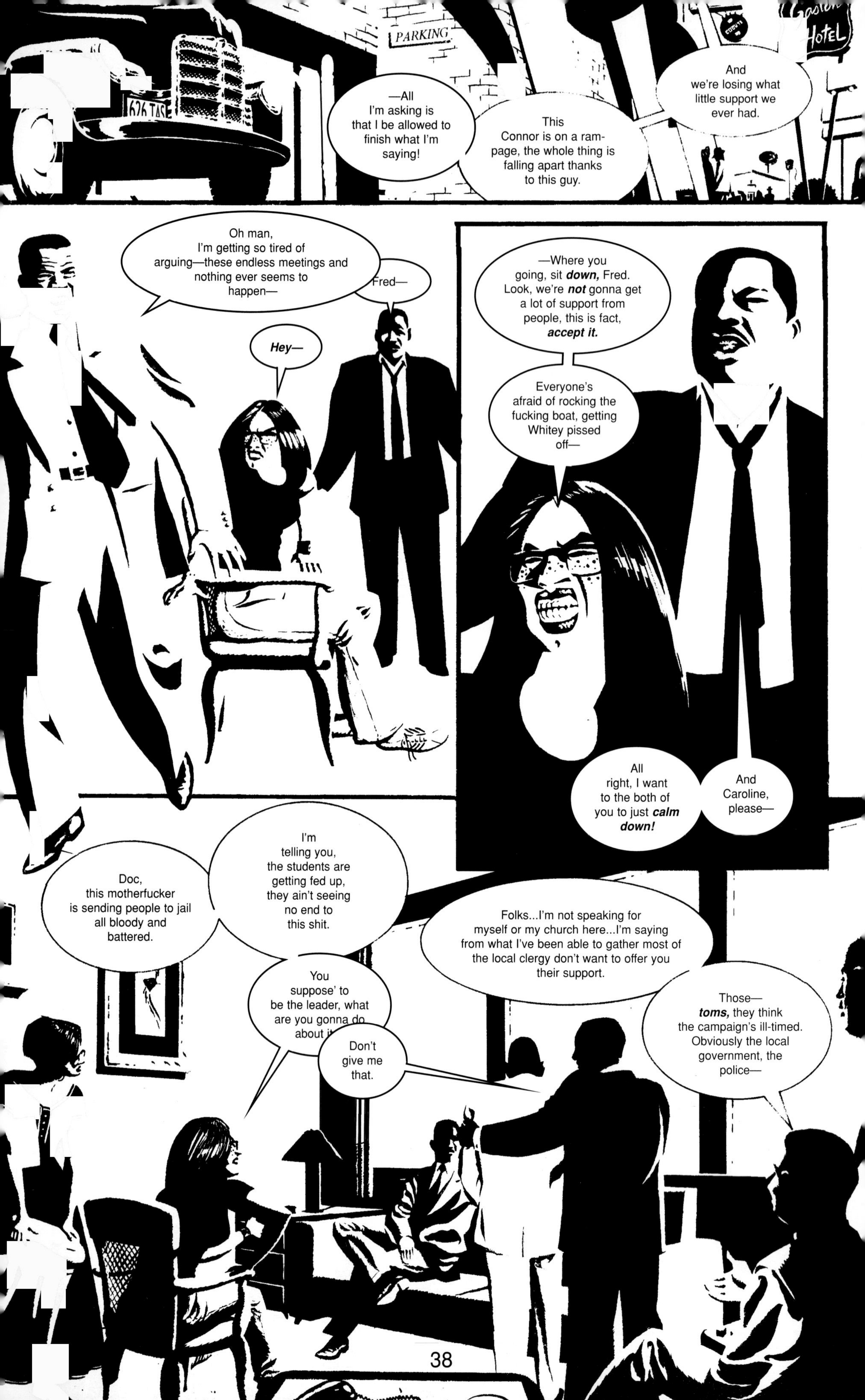
PARKING
626 TAS
HOTEL
—All I'm asking is that I be allowed to finish what I'm saying!
This Connor is on a ram-page, the whole thing is falling apart thanks to this guy.
And we're losing what little support we ever had.
Oh man, I'm getting so tired of arguing—these endless meetings and nothing ever seems to happen—
Fred—
Hey—
—Where you going, sit ***down,*** Fred. Look, we're ***not*** gonna get a lot of support from people, this is fact, ***accept it.***
Everyone's afraid of rocking the fucking boat, getting Whitey pissed off—
All right, I want to the both of you to just ***calm down!***
And Caroline, please—
Doc, this motherfucker is sending people to jail all bloody and battered.
I'm telling you, the students are getting fed up, they ain't seeing no end to this shit.
You suppose' to be the leader, what are you gonna do about it
Don't give me that.
Folks...I'm not speaking for myself or my church here...I'm saying from what I've been able to gather most of the local clergy don't want to offer you their support.
Those— ***toms,*** they think the campaign's ill-timed. Obviously the local government, the police—

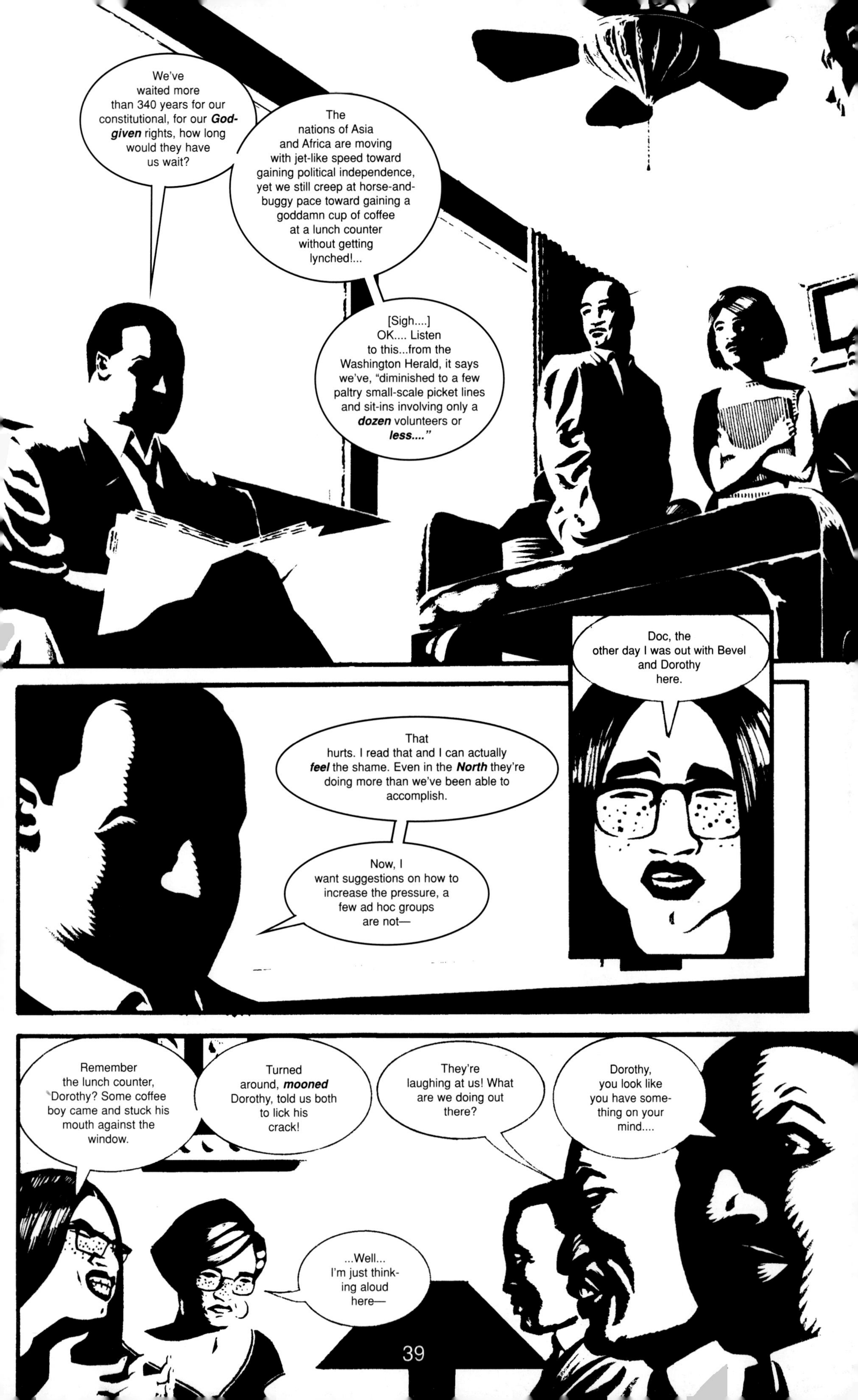
We've waited more than 340 years for our constitutional, for our ***God-given*** rights, how long would they have us wait?
The nations of Asia and Africa are moving with jet-like speed toward gaining political independence, yet we still creep at horse-and-buggy pace toward gaining a goddamn cup of coffee at a lunch counter without getting lynched!...
[Sigh....] OK.... Listen to this...from the Washington Herald, it says we've, "diminished to a few paltry small-scale picket lines and sit-ins involving only a ***dozen*** volunteers or ***less....***"
Doc, the other day I was out with Bevel and Dorothy here.
That hurts. I read that and I can actually ***feel*** the shame. Even in the ***North*** they're doing more than we've been able to accomplish.
Now, I want suggestions on how to increase the pressure, a few ad hoc groups are not—
Remember the lunch counter, Dorothy? Some coffee boy came and stuck his mouth against the window.
Turned around, ***mooned*** Dorothy, told us both to lick his crack!
They're laughing at us! What are we doing out there?
Dorothy, you look like you have something on your mind....
...Well... I'm just thinking aloud here—

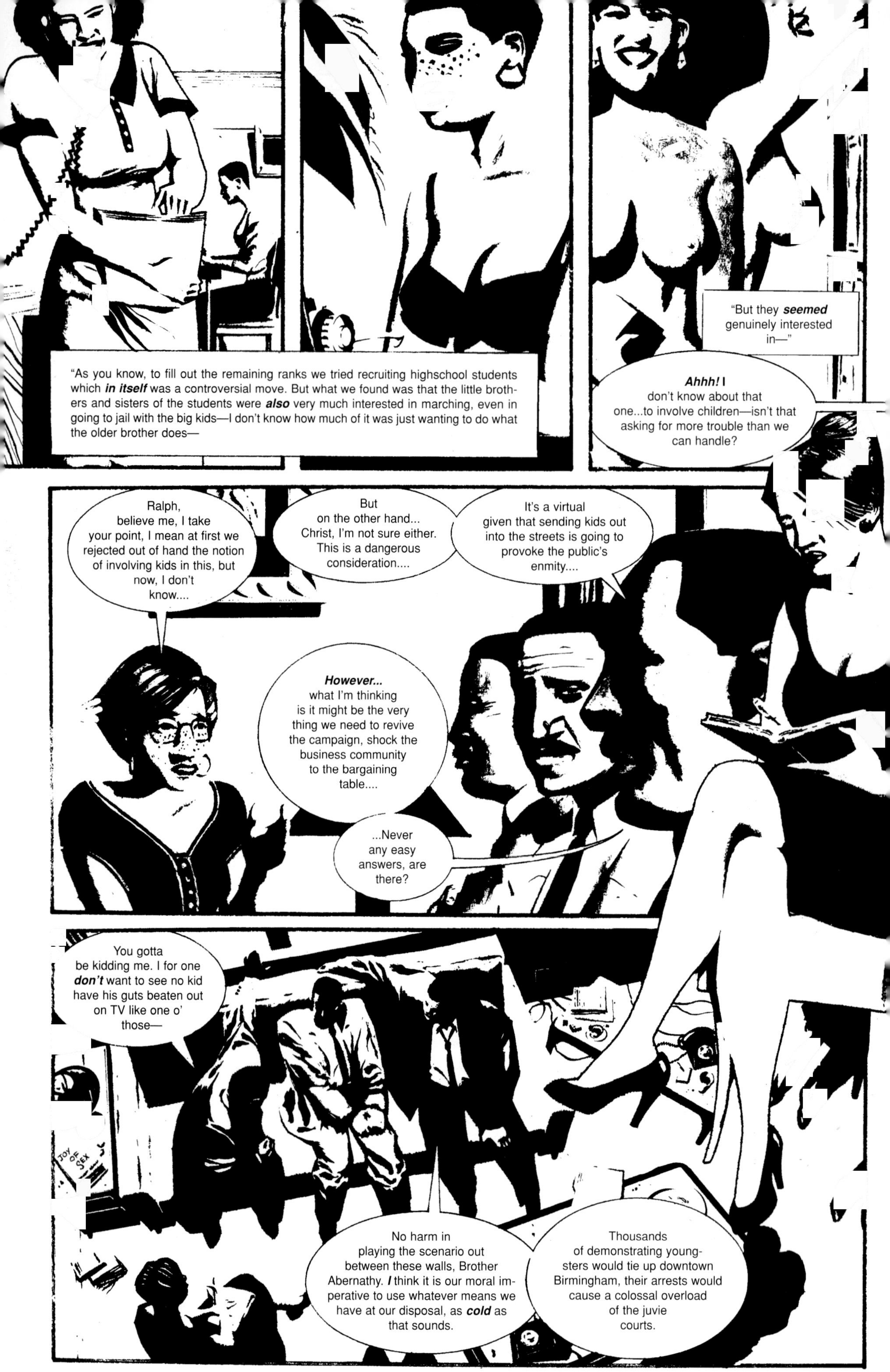
"As you know, to fill out the remaining ranks we tried recruiting highschool students which ***in itself*** was a controversial move. But what we found was that the little brothers and sisters of the students were ***also*** very much interested in marching, even in going to jail with the big kids—I don't know how much of it was just wanting to do what the older brother does—
"But they ***seemed*** genuinely interested in—"
Ahhh! I don't know about that one...to involve children—isn't that asking for more trouble than we can handle?
Ralph, believe me, I take your point, I mean at first we rejected out of hand the notion of involving kids in this, but now, I don't know....
But on the other hand... Christ, I'm not sure either. This is a dangerous consideration....
It's a virtual given that sending kids out into the streets is going to provoke the public's enmity....
However... what I'm thinking is it might be the very thing we need to revive the campaign, shock the business community to the bargaining table....
...Never any easy answers, are there?
You gotta be kidding me. I for one ***don't*** want to see no kid have his guts beaten out on TV like one o' those—
JOY OF SEX
No harm in playing the scenario out between these walls, Brother Abernathy. ***I*** think it is our moral imperative to use whatever means we have at our disposal, as ***cold*** as that sounds.
Thousands of demonstrating youngsters would tie up downtown Birmingham, their arrests would cause a colossal overload of the juvie courts.

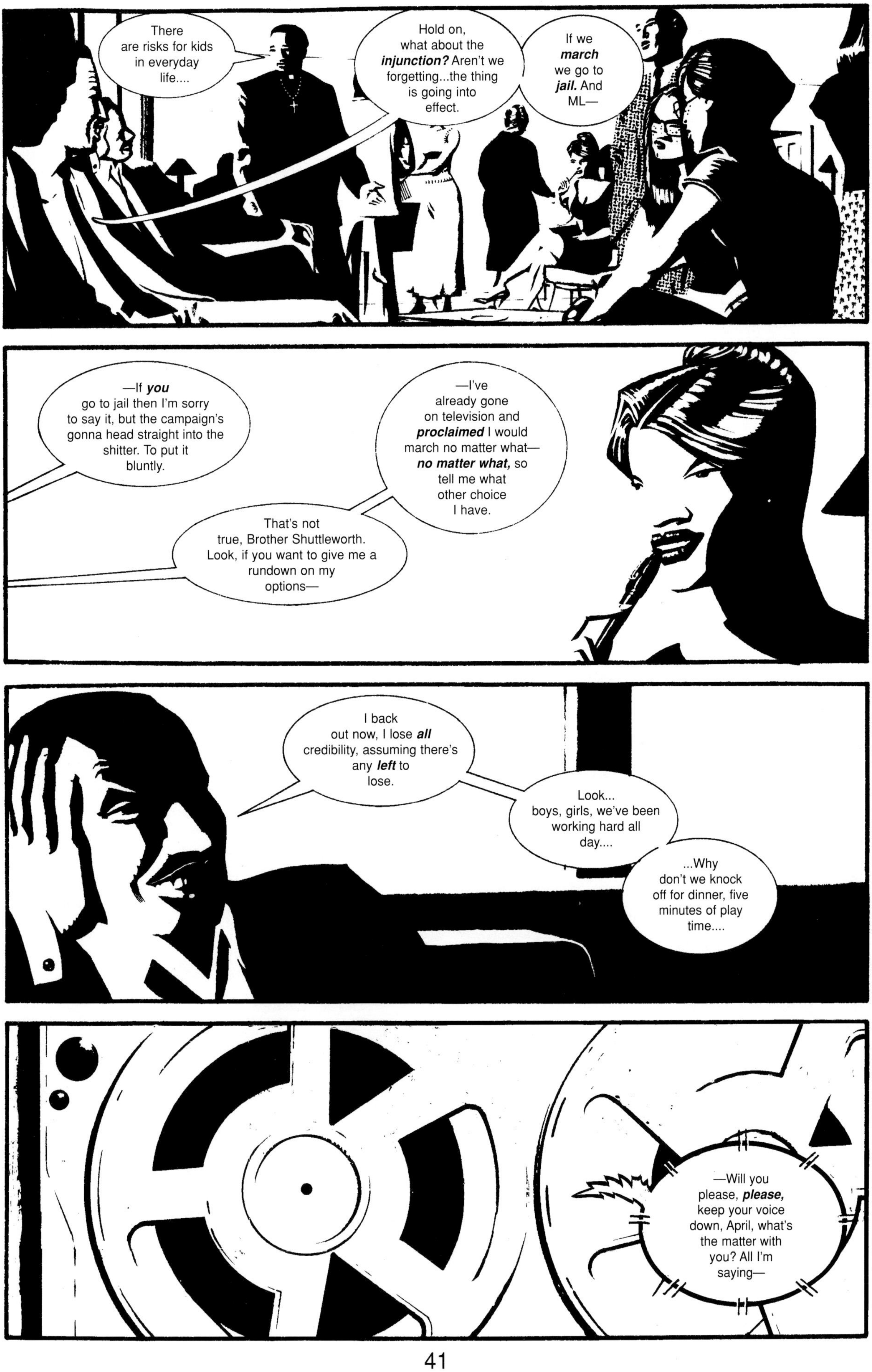
There are risks for kids in everyday life....
Hold on, what about the *injunction?* Aren't we forgetting...the thing is going into effect.
If we *march* we go to *jail.* And ML—
—If *you* go to jail then I'm sorry to say it, but the campaign's gonna head straight into the shitter. To put it bluntly.
—I've already gone on television and *proclaimed* I would march no matter what— *no matter what,* so tell me what other choice I have.
That's not true, Brother Shuttleworth. Look, if you want to give me a rundown on my options—
I back out now, I lose *all* credibility, assuming there's any *left* to lose.
Look... boys, girls, we've been working hard all day....
...Why don't we knock off for dinner, five minutes of play time....
—Will you please, *please,* keep your voice down, April, what's the matter with you? All I'm saying—

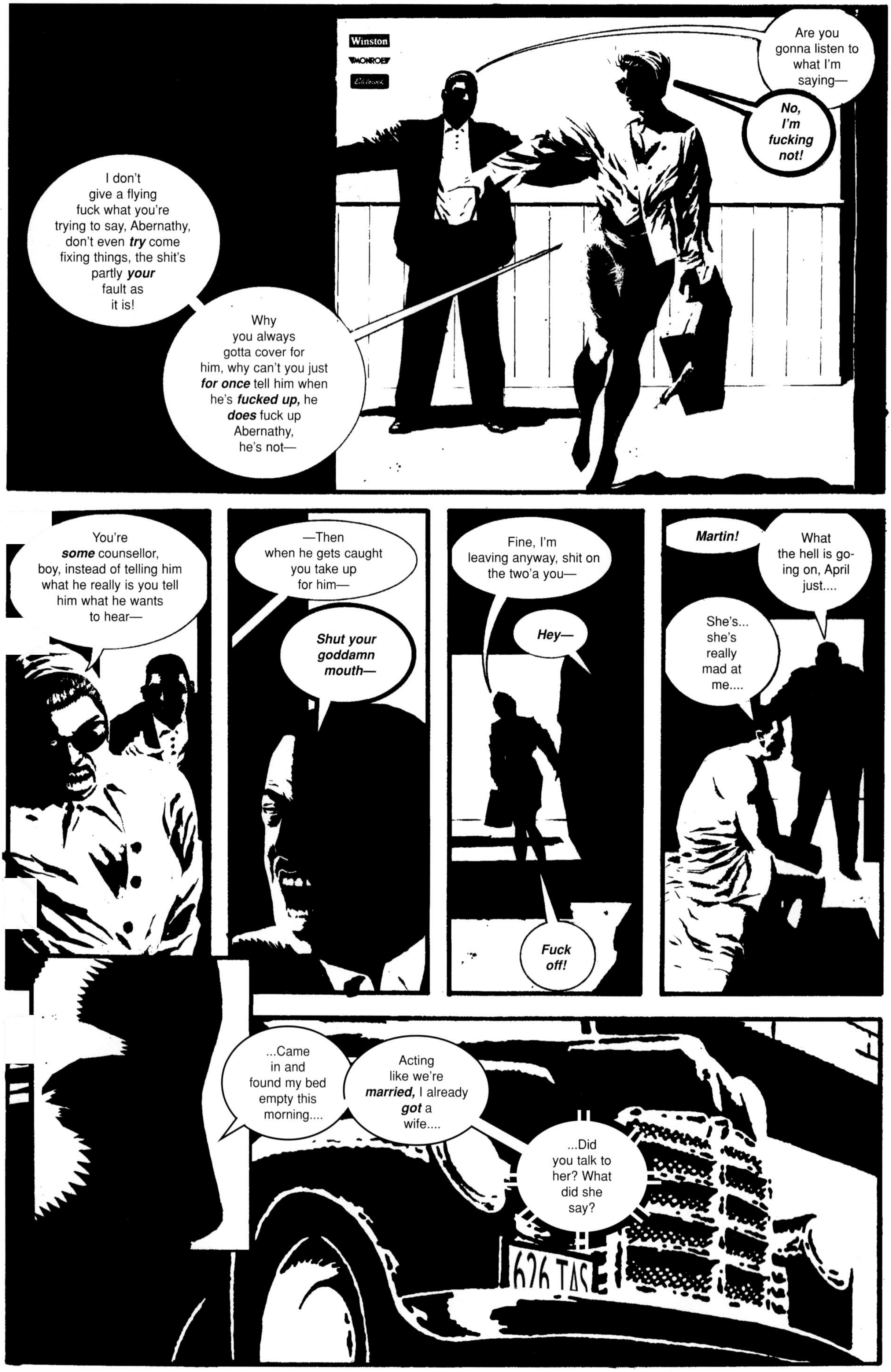
Winston
MONROE
Are you gonna listen to what I'm saying—
No, I'm fucking not!
I don't give a flying fuck what you're trying to say, Abernathy, don't even try come fixing things, the shit's partly your fault as it is!
Why you always gotta cover for him, why can't you just for once tell him when he's fucked up, he does fuck up Abernathy, he's not—
You're some counsellor, boy, instead of telling him what he really is you tell him what he wants to hear—
—Then when he gets caught you take up for him—
Shut your goddamn mouth—
Fine, I'm leaving anyway, shit on the two'a you—
Hey—
Fuck off!
Martin!
What the hell is going on, April just....
She's... she's really mad at me....
...Came in and found my bed empty this morning....
Acting like we're married, I already got a wife....
...Did you talk to her? What did she say?
626 TAS

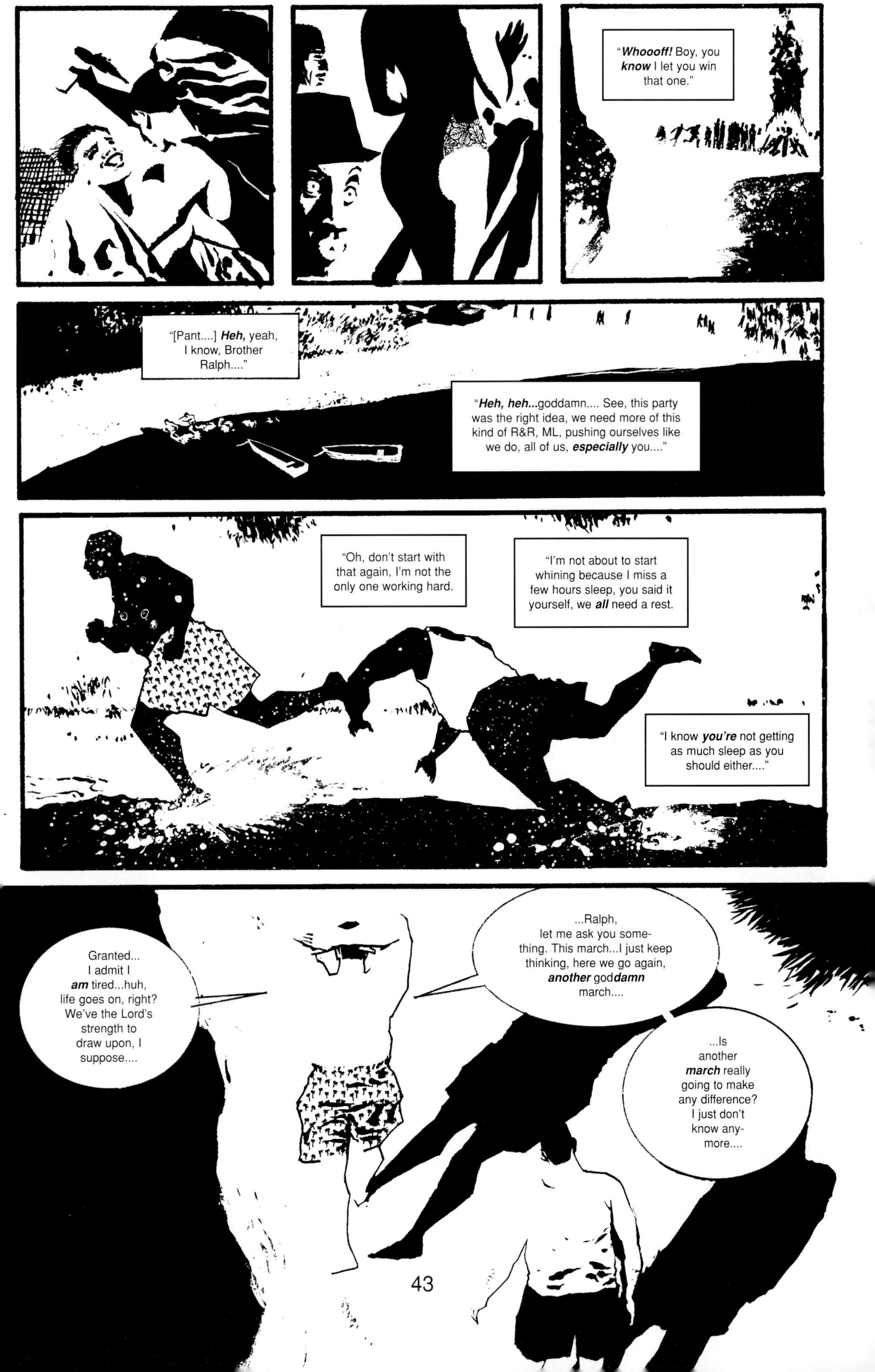
"**Whoooff!** Boy, you **know** I let you win that one."
"[Pant....] **Heh,** yeah, I know, Brother Ralph...."
"**Heh, heh...**goddamn.... See, this party was the right idea, we need more of this kind of R&R, ML, pushing ourselves like we do, all of us, **especially** you...."
"Oh, don't start with that again, I'm not the only one working hard.
"I'm not about to start whining because I miss a few hours sleep, you said it yourself, we **all** need a rest.
"I know **you're** not getting as much sleep as you should either...."
...Ralph, let me ask you something. This march...I just keep thinking, here we go again, **another** god**damn** march....
Granted... I admit I **am** tired...huh, life goes on, right? We've the Lord's strength to draw upon, I suppose....
...Is another **march** really going to make any difference? I just don't know anymore....

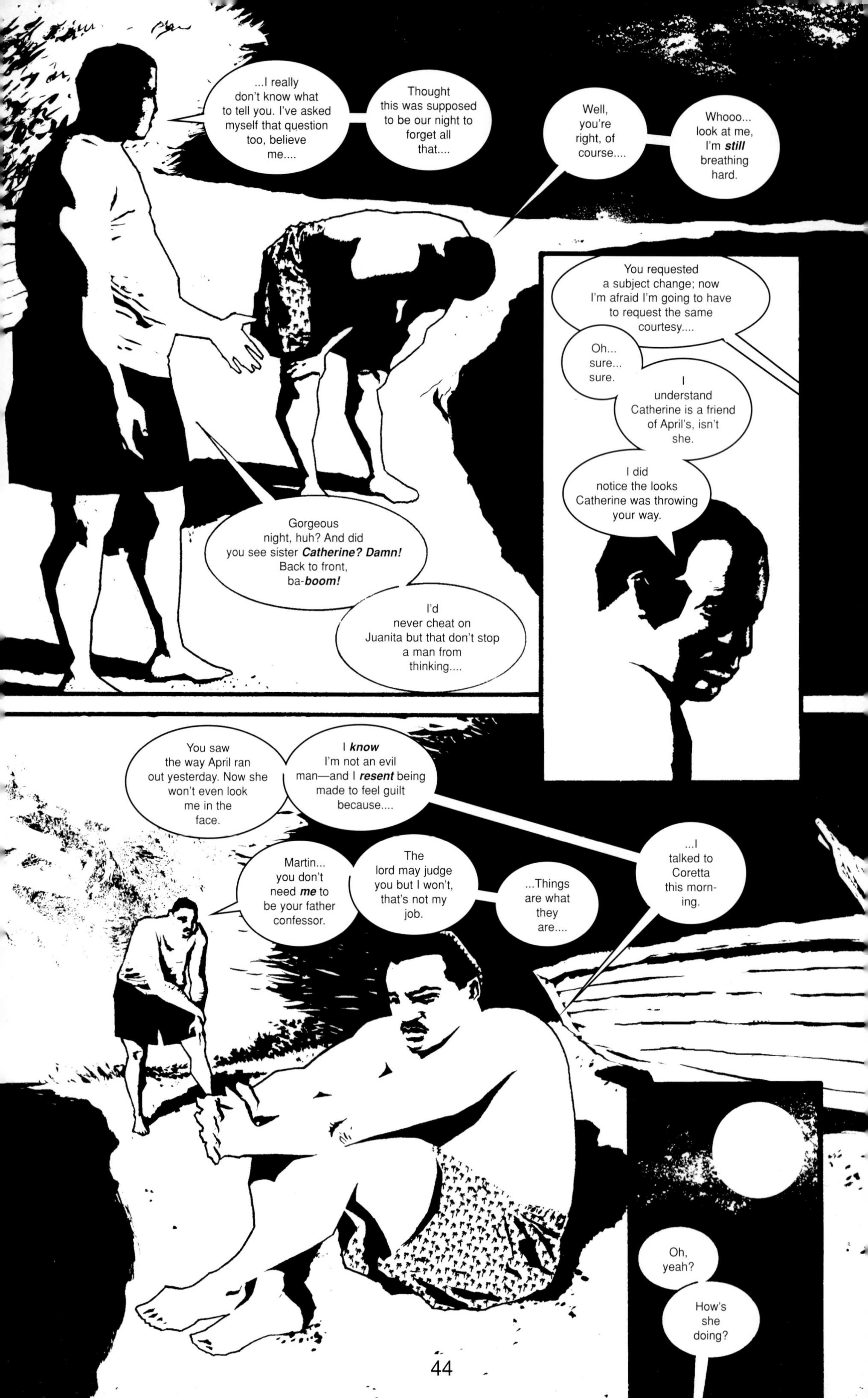
...I really don't know what to tell you. I've asked myself that question too, believe me....
Thought this was supposed to be our night to forget all that....
Well, you're right, of course....
Whooo... look at me, I'm ***still*** breathing hard.
Gorgeous night, huh? And did you see sister ***Catherine? Damn!*** Back to front, ba-***boom!***
I'd never cheat on Juanita but that don't stop a man from thinking....
You requested a subject change; now I'm afraid I'm going to have to request the same courtesy....
Oh... sure... sure.
I understand Catherine is a friend of April's, isn't she.
I did notice the looks Catherine was throwing your way.
You saw the way April ran out yesterday. Now she won't even look me in the face.
I ***know*** I'm not an evil man—and I ***resent*** being made to feel guilt because....
Martin... you don't need ***me*** to be your father confessor.
The lord may judge you but I won't, that's not my job.
...Things are what they are....
...I talked to Coretta this morn-ing.
Oh, yeah?
How's she doing?

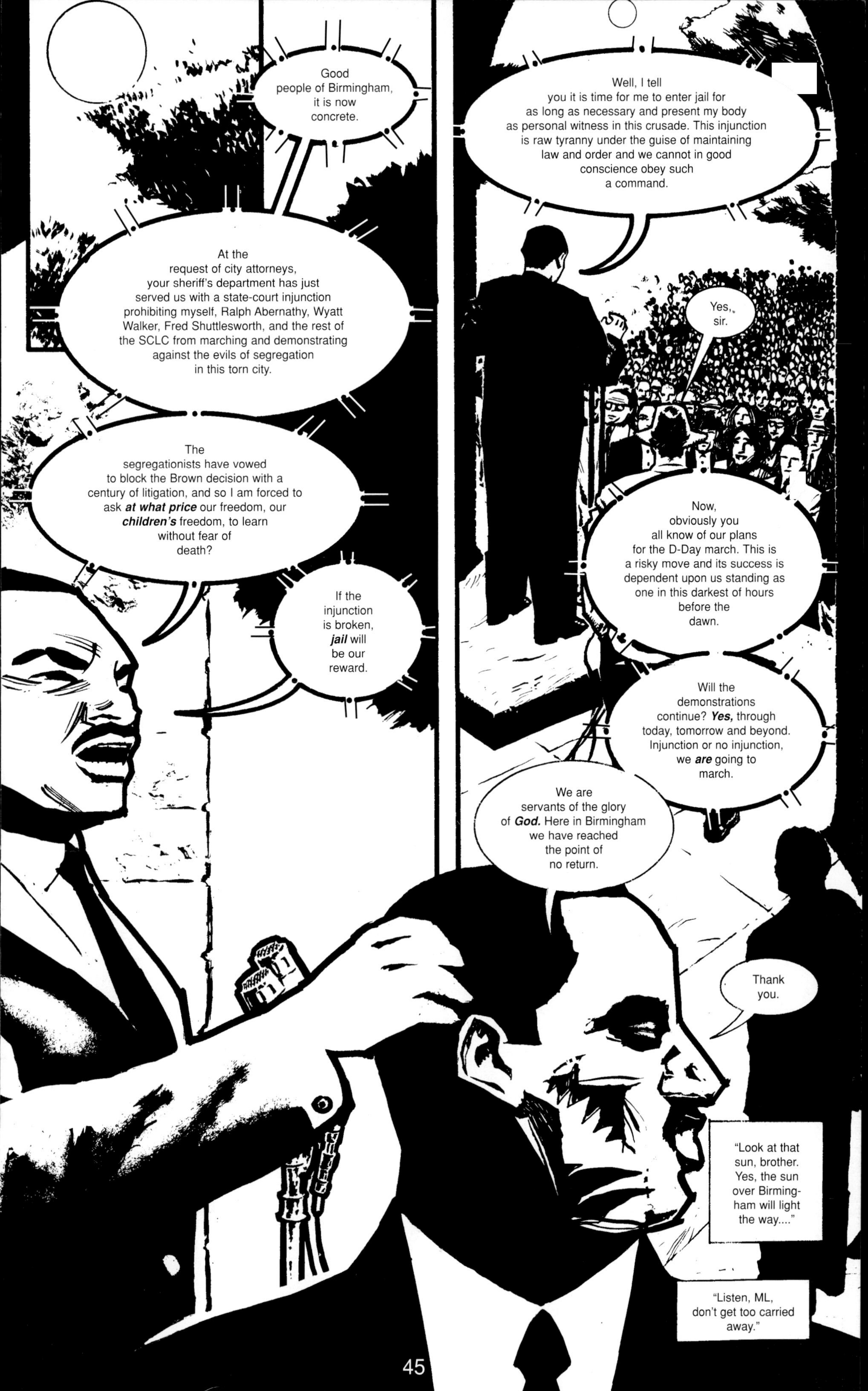

Good people of Birmingham, it is now concrete.
At the request of city attorneys, your sheriff's department has just served us with a state-court injunction prohibiting myself, Ralph Abernathy, Wyatt Walker, Fred Shuttlesworth, and the rest of the SCLC from marching and demonstrating against the evils of segregation in this torn city.
The segregationists have vowed to block the Brown decision with a century of litigation, and so I am forced to ask ***at what price*** our freedom, our ***children's*** freedom, to learn without fear of death?
If the injunction is broken, ***jail*** will be our reward.
Well, I tell you it is time for me to enter jail for as long as necessary and present my body as personal witness in this crusade. This injunction is raw tyranny under the guise of maintaining law and order and we cannot in good conscience obey such a command.
Yes, sir.
Now, obviously you all know of our plans for the D-Day march. This is a risky move and its success is dependent upon us standing as one in this darkest of hours before the dawn.
Will the demonstrations continue? ***Yes,*** through today, tomorrow and beyond. Injunction or no injunction, we ***are*** going to march.
We are servants of the glory of ***God.*** Here in Birmingham we have reached the point of no return.
Thank you.
"Look at that sun, brother. Yes, the sun over Birmingham will light the way...."
"Listen, ML, don't get too carried away."

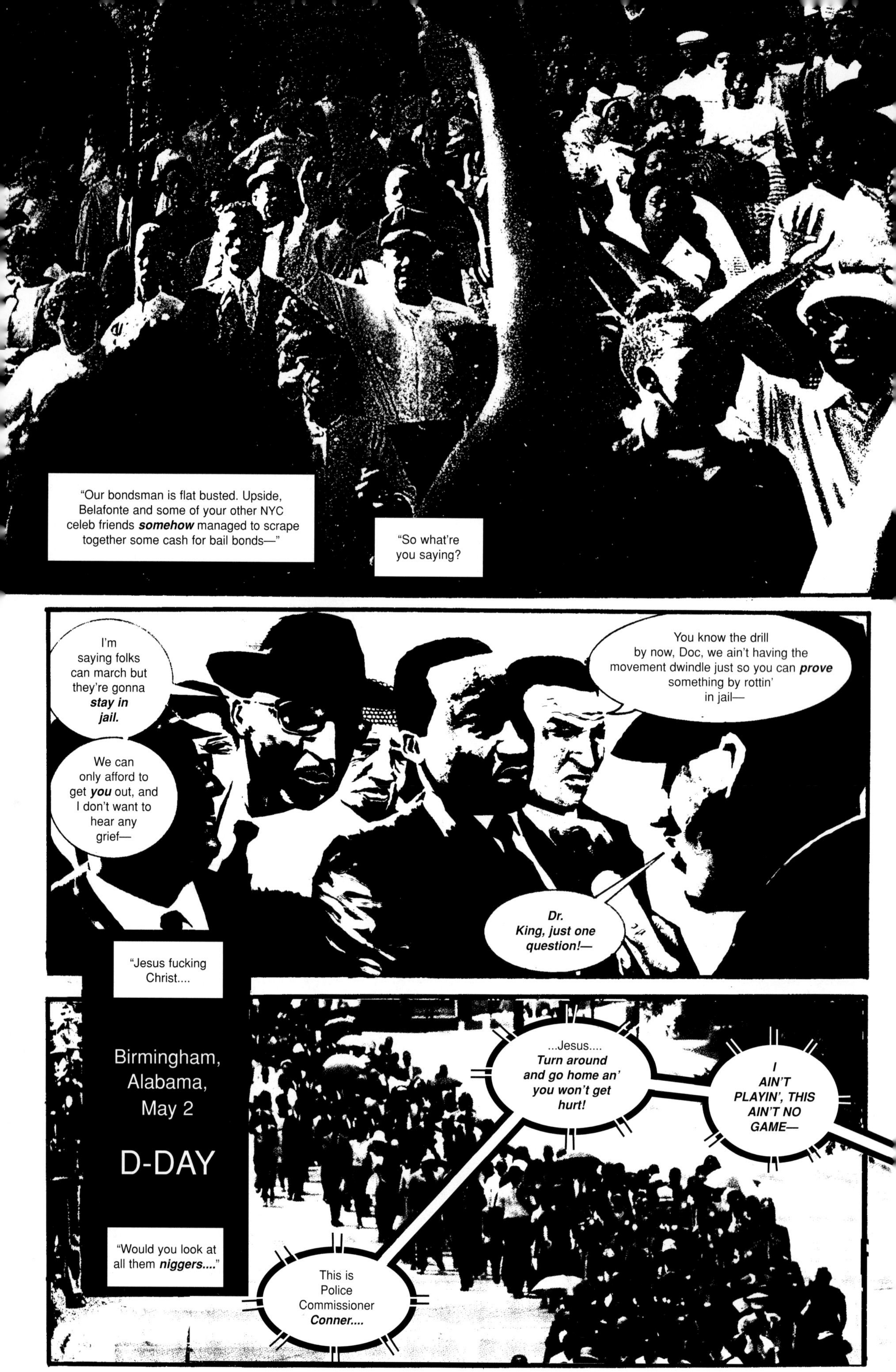
"Our bondsman is flat busted. Upside, Belafonte and some of your other NYC celeb friends ***somehow*** managed to scrape together some cash for bail bonds—"
"So what're you saying?
I'm saying folks can march but they're gonna ***stay in jail.***
We can only afford to get ***you*** out, and I don't want to hear any grief—
You know the drill by now, Doc, we ain't having the movement dwindle just so you can ***prove*** something by rottin' in jail—
Dr. King, just one question!—
"Jesus fucking Christ....
Birmingham, Alabama, May 2
D-DAY
"Would you look at all them ***niggers....***"
This is Police Commissioner ***Conner....***
...Jesus.... ***Turn around and go home an' you won't get hurt!***
I AIN'T PLAYIN', THIS AIN'T NO GAME—

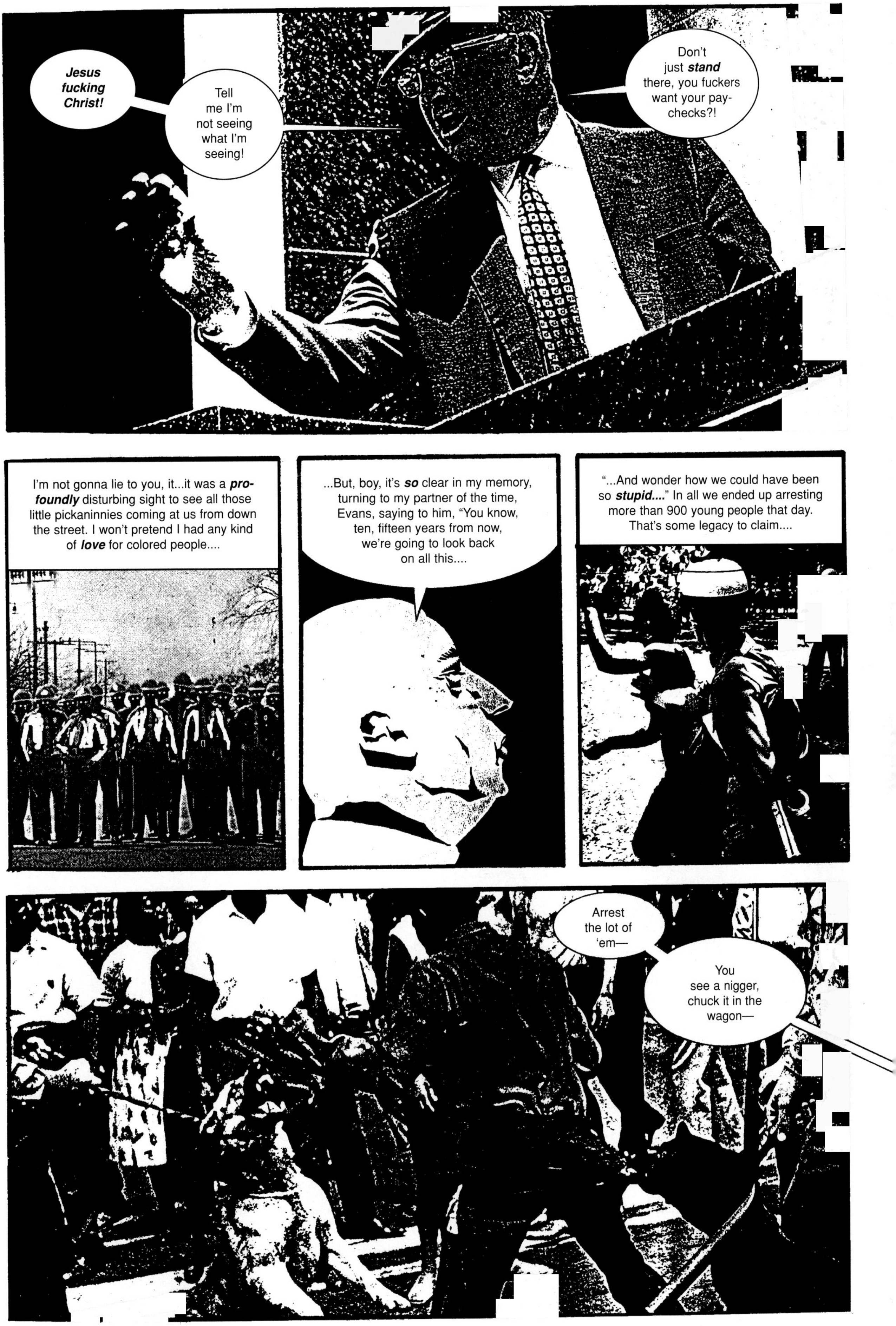

Jesus fucking Christ!
Tell me I'm not seeing what I'm seeing!
Don't just stand there, you fuckers want your pay-checks?!
I'm not gonna lie to you, it...it was a pro-foundly disturbing sight to see all those little pickaninnies coming at us from down the street. I won't pretend I had any kind of love for colored people....
...But, boy, it's so clear in my memory, turning to my partner of the time, Evans, saying to him, "You know, ten, fifteen years from now, we're going to look back on all this....
"...And wonder how we could have been so stupid...." In all we ended up arresting more than 900 young people that day. That's some legacy to claim....
Arrest the lot of 'em—
You see a nigger, chuck it in the wagon—

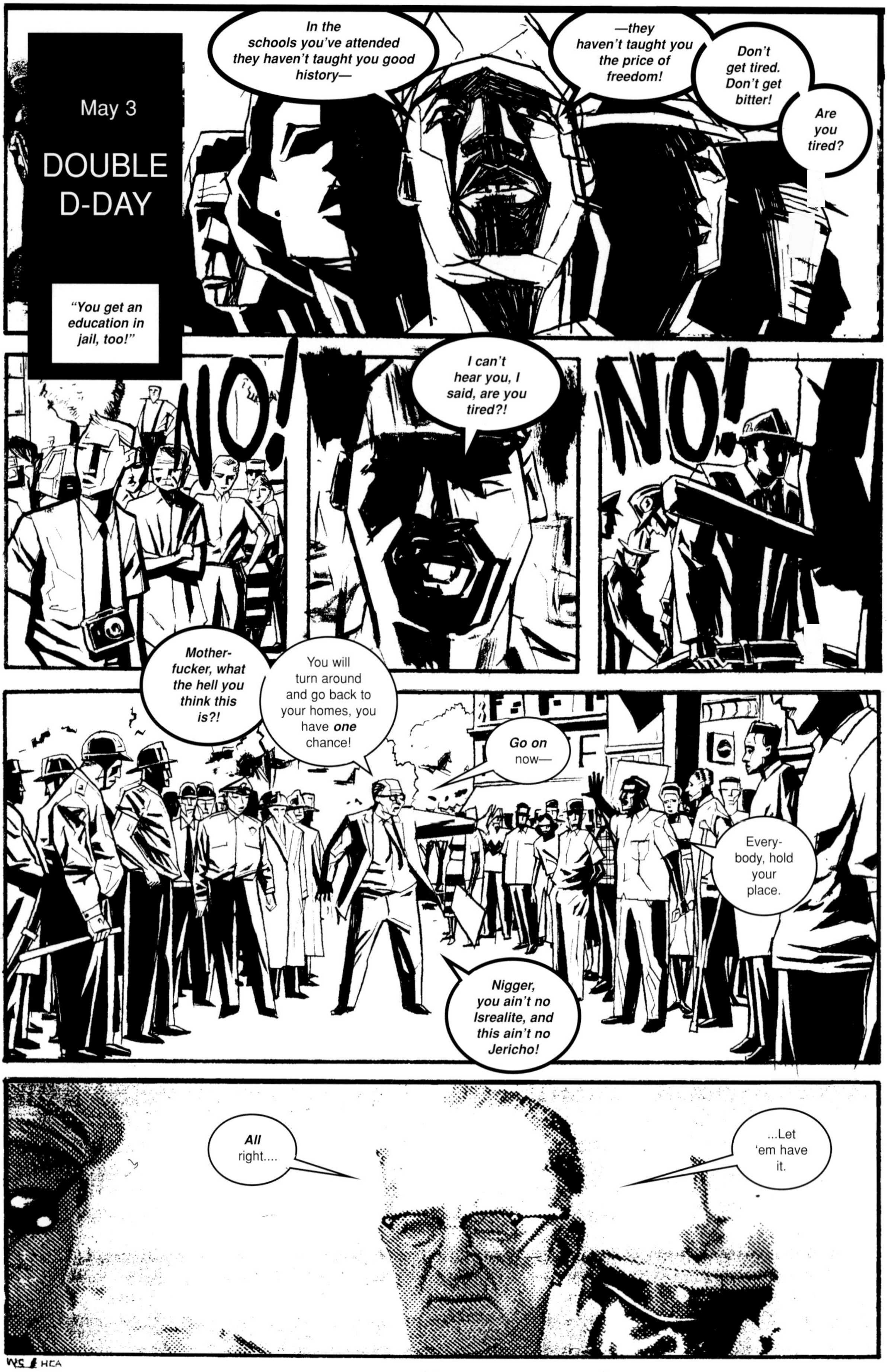
May 3
DOUBLE D-DAY
"You get an education in jail, too!"
In the schools you've attended they haven't taught you good history—
—they haven't taught you the price of freedom!
Don't get tired. Don't get bitter!
Are you tired?
NO!
I can't hear you, I said, are you tired?!
NO!
Mother-fucker, what the hell you think this is?!
You will turn around and go back to your homes, you have one chance!
Go on now—
Every-body, hold your place.
Nigger, you ain't no Isrealite, and this ain't no Jericho!
All right....
...Let 'em have it.

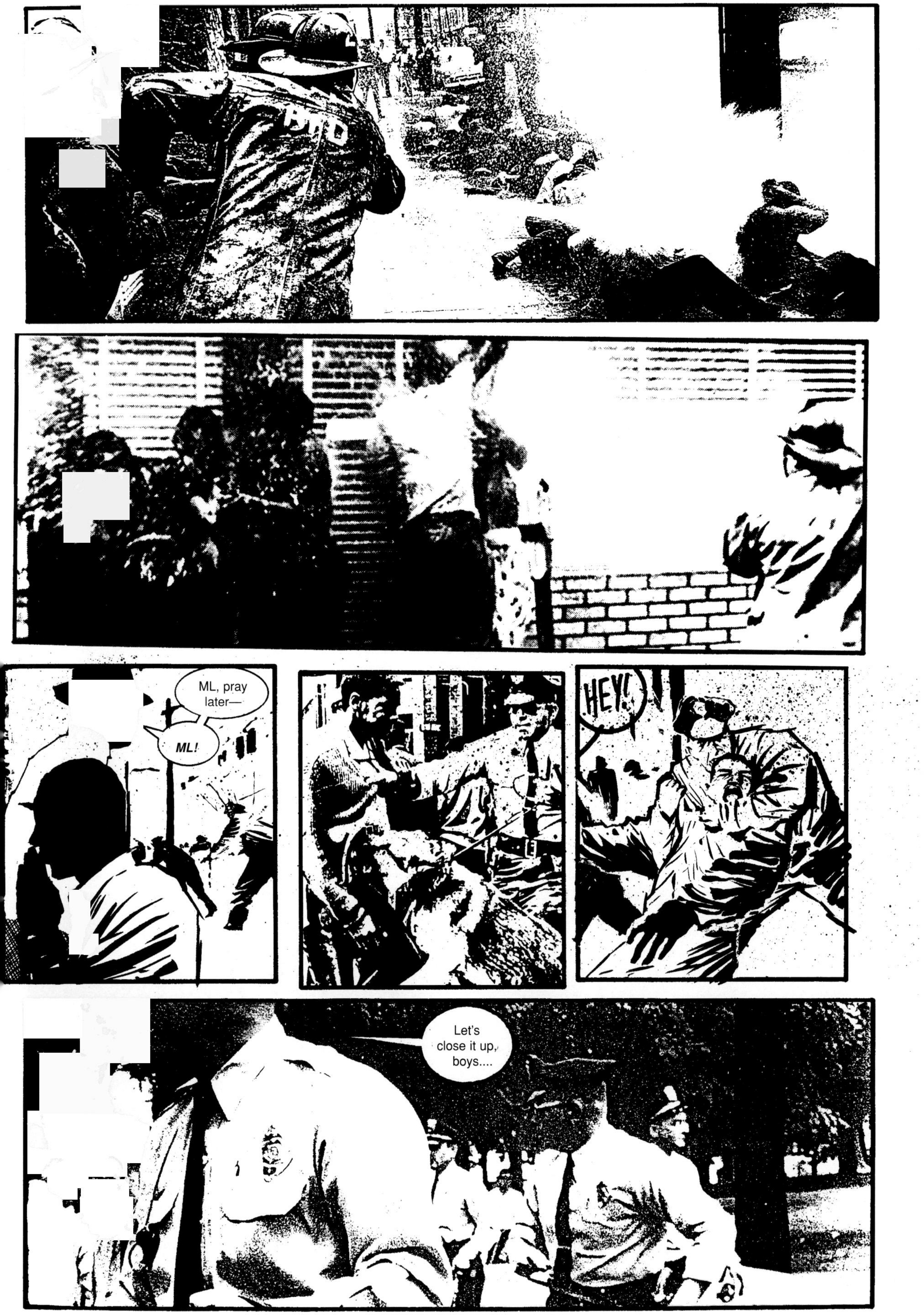
ML, pray later—
ML!
HEY!
Let's close it up, boys....

Martin King said, "Don't worry about your children in jail. The eyes of the world are on Birmingham." ...And he was right.

To see the photos of that mayhem, my kids and myself looking at them in the morning paper, and then that evening on the news.... You have to wonder what it must *feel* like to be driven to that level of violence.

I never told anyone growing up I was half-negro, not even my husband, somehow I managed to pass. He's a good man, my husband...we tried to teach our kids differently, to say *colored* or *afro-American,* never that other word....

"How long we gotta put up with this **bull**shit? What, we gotta start **killing** people like Bull Connor?"

DOGS RELEASED ON INGRAM PARK PROTESTORS

By Junior Kirkpatrick

"Connor, you all right, man, you doing the right thing."

Frankly, what I saw in the papers made me sick. But unfortunately there's nothing I can legally do at this time to restrain Connor. ...In all candor, both the attorney general and myself feel the timing of this campaign—

"—Could have been handled with greater sensitivity. That said, we're not asking Dr. King or any of the other Negro leaders for patience. We can well understand why the Blacks of Birmingham have reached the limits of their patience.

CONNOR ON THE RAMPAGE

who reportedly saw Connor on a Jim Bean date with an underage blonde in Vegas! Now, we're not usually ones for gossip, but c'mon, you get a story like that you tell me *you're* not gonna print it? Yeah, right. Listen, don't get all moral on me, we got reporters, we know where you live, we can find stuff out real easy-like, so keep your nose clean, nimrod.

Fellow Americans, this nation was founded on the principle that all men are created equal, that the rights of every man are diminished when the rights of one man are threatened. Every American has the right to attend any public institution, enjoy equal service in any

public facility, and register and vote without having to take to the streets or call for federal troops. We are confronted primarily with a moral issue as old as the scriptures and as dear as the American con-stitution: whether all Americans are to be afforded equal rights

and equal opportunities. We claim we're the land of the free, and we are, except for Negroes. The time has come for America to remove the blight of racial discrimination and fulfill her brilliant promise.

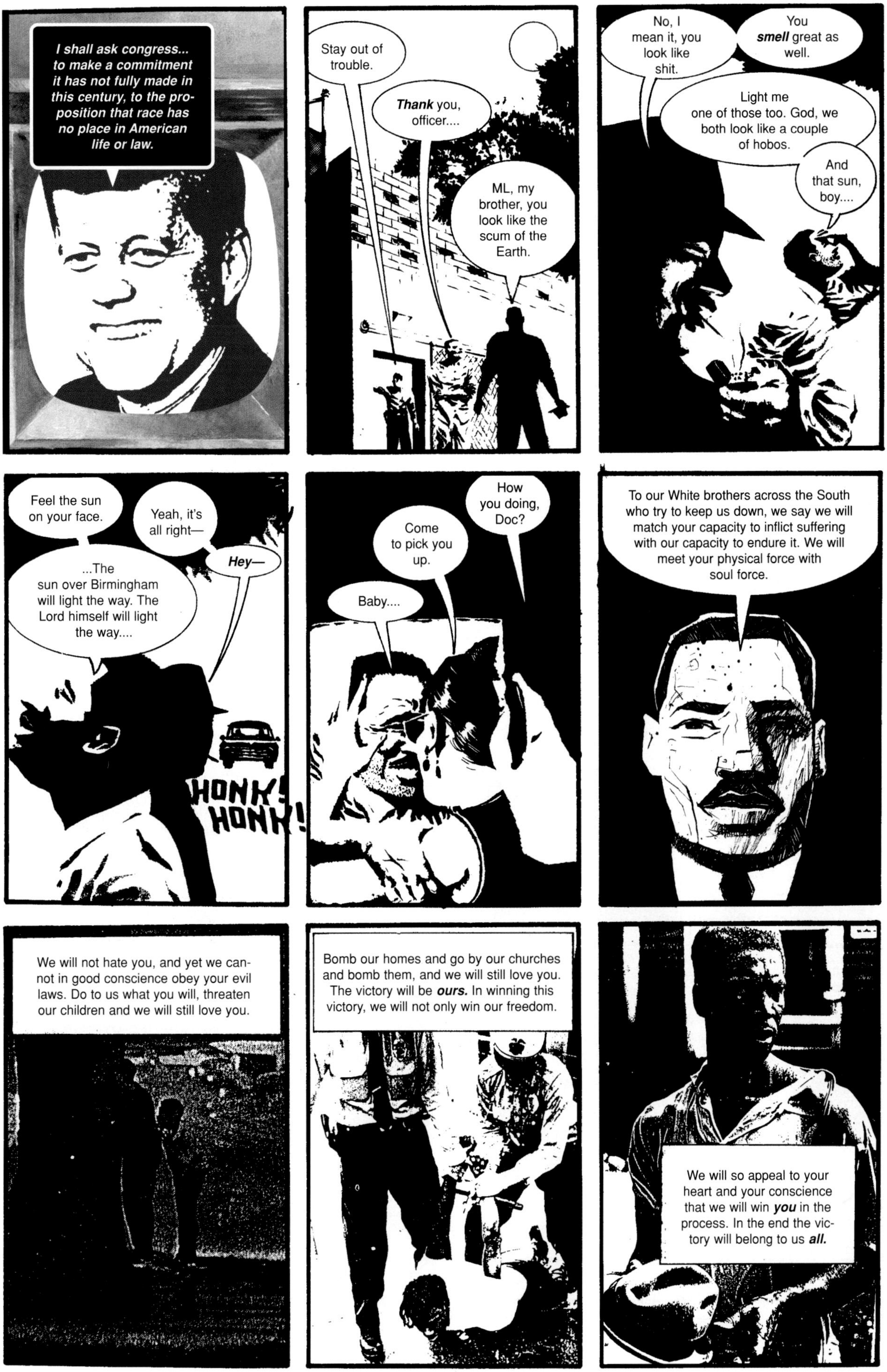

I shall ask congress... to make a commitment it has not fully made in this century, to the proposition that race has no place in American life or law.
Stay out of trouble.
Thank you, officer....
ML, my brother, you look like the scum of the Earth.
No, I mean it, you look like shit.
You smell great as well.
Light me one of those too. God, we both look like a couple of hobos.
And that sun, boy....
Feel the sun on your face.
Yeah, it's all right—
...The sun over Birmingham will light the way. The Lord himself will light the way....
Hey—
HONK! HONK!
How you doing, Doc?
Come to pick you up.
Baby....
To our White brothers across the South who try to keep us down, we say we will match your capacity to inflict suffering with our capacity to endure it. We will meet your physical force with soul force.
We will not hate you, and yet we cannot in good conscience obey your evil laws. Do to us what you will, threaten our children and we will still love you.
Bomb our homes and go by our churches and bomb them, and we will still love you. The victory will be ours. In winning this victory, we will not only win our freedom.
We will so appeal to your heart and your conscience that we will win you in the process. In the end the victory will belong to us all.

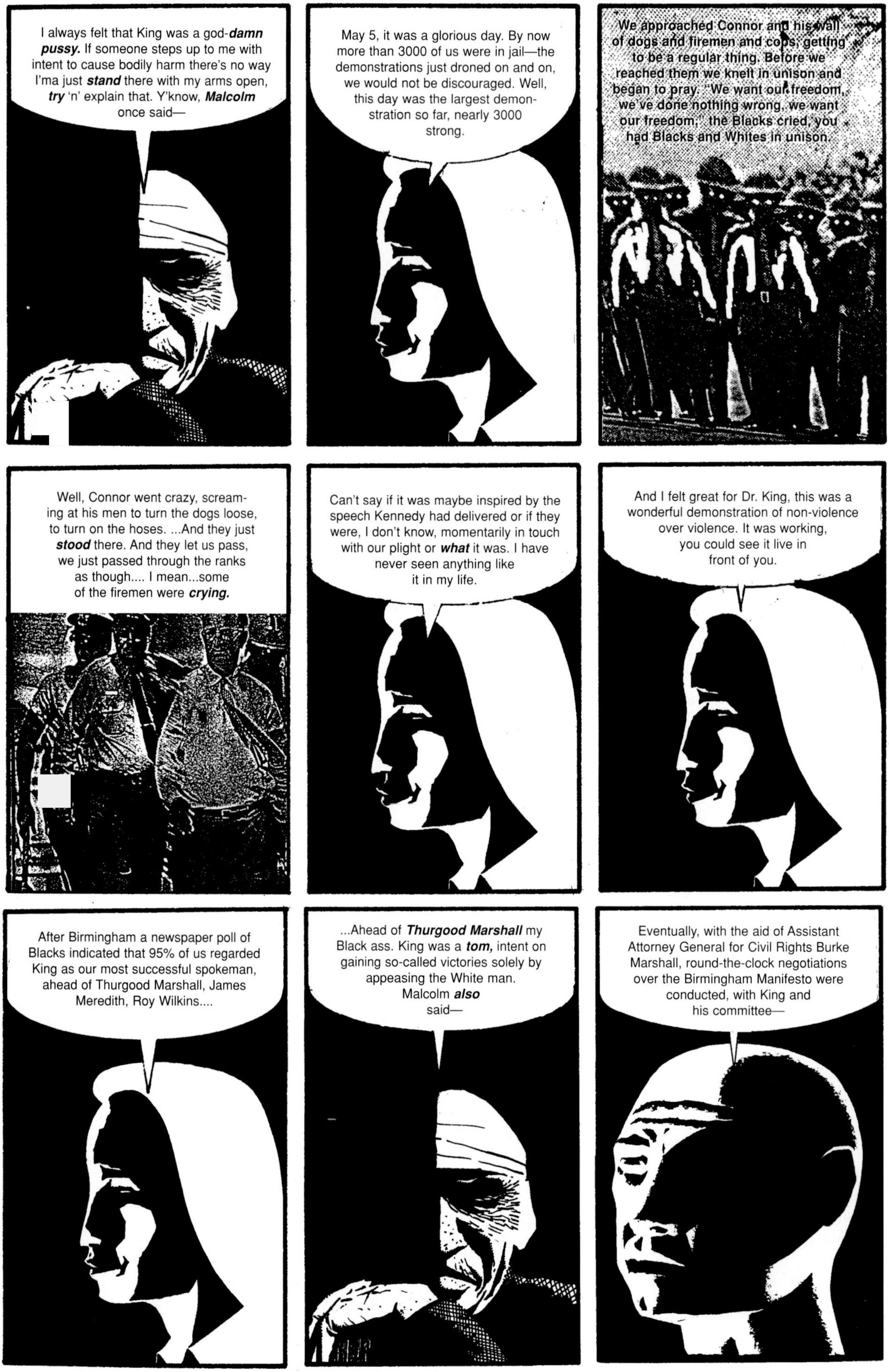
I always felt that King was a god-***damn pussy.*** If someone steps up to me with intent to cause bodily harm there's no way I'ma just ***stand*** there with my arms open, ***try*** 'n' explain that. Y'know, ***Malcolm*** once said—
May 5, it was a glorious day. By now more than 3000 of us were in jail—the demonstrations just droned on and on, we would not be discouraged. Well, this day was the largest demonstration so far, nearly 3000 strong.
We approached Connor and his wall of dogs and firemen and cops, getting to be a regular thing. Before we reached them we knelt in unison and began to pray. "We want our freedom, we've done nothing wrong, we want our freedom," the Blacks cried, you had Blacks and Whites in unison.
Well, Connor went crazy, screaming at his men to turn the dogs loose, to turn on the hoses. ...And they just ***stood*** there. And they let us pass, we just passed through the ranks as though.... I mean...some of the firemen were ***crying.***
Can't say if it was maybe inspired by the speech Kennedy had delivered or if they were, I don't know, momentarily in touch with our plight or ***what*** it was. I have never seen anything like it in my life.
And I felt great for Dr. King, this was a wonderful demonstration of non-violence over violence. It was working, you could see it live in front of you.
After Birmingham a newspaper poll of Blacks indicated that 95% of us regarded King as our most successful spokeman, ahead of Thurgood Marshall, James Meredith, Roy Wilkins....
...Ahead of ***Thurgood Marshall*** my Black ass. King was a ***tom,*** intent on gaining so-called victories solely by appeasing the White man. Malcolm ***also*** said—
Eventually, with the aid of Assistant Attorney General for Civil Rights Burke Marshall, round-the-clock negotiations over the Birmingham Manifesto were conducted, with King and his committee—

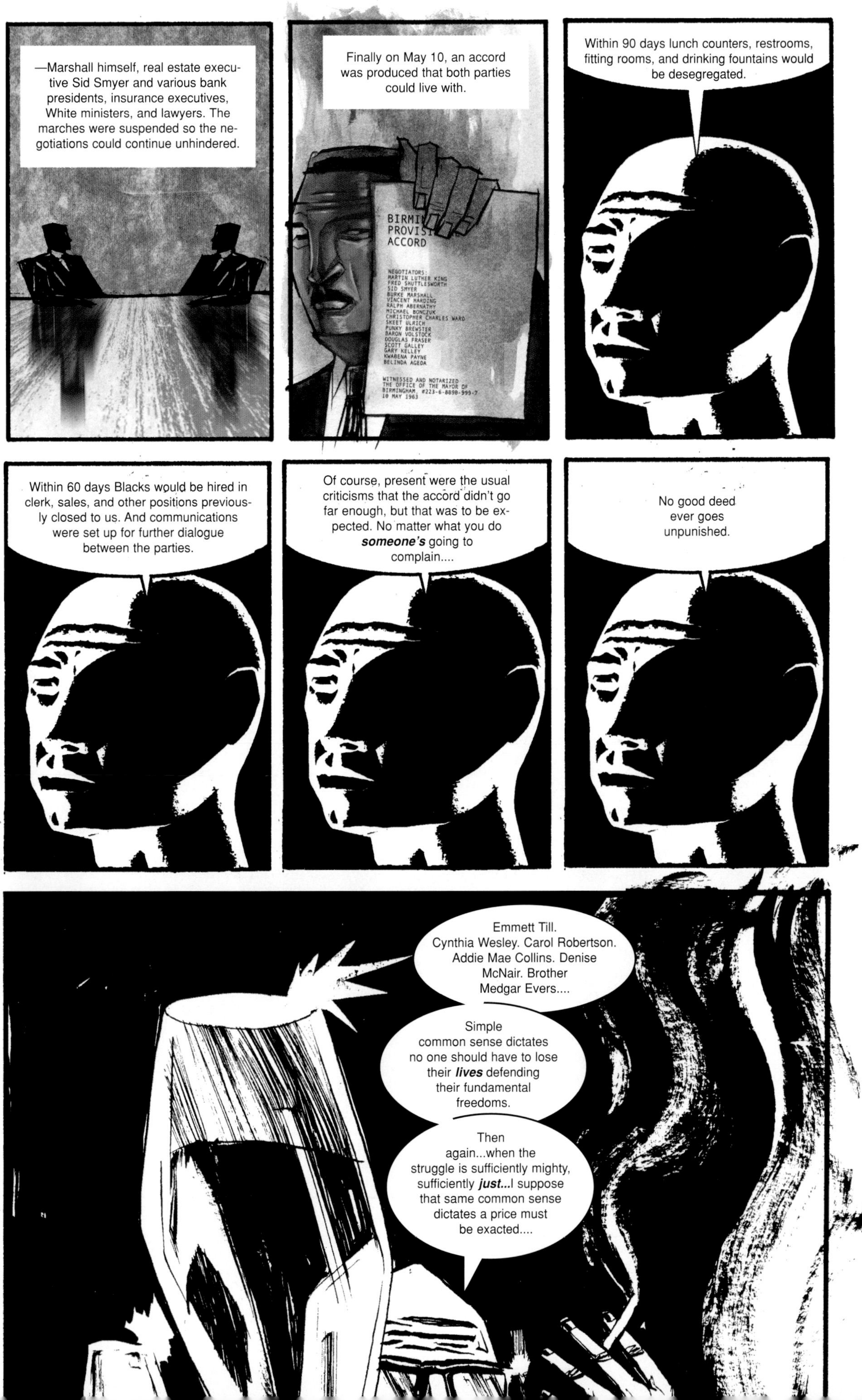
—Marshall himself, real estate executive Sid Smyer and various bank presidents, insurance executives, White ministers, and lawyers. The marches were suspended so the negotiations could continue unhindered.
Finally on May 10, an accord was produced that both parties could live with.
ACCORD
NEGOTIATORS:
MARTIN LUTHER KING
FRED SHUTTLESWORTH
SID SMYER
BURKE MARSHALL
VINCENT HARDING
RALPH ABERNATHY
MICHAEL BONCZUK
CHRISTOPHER CHARLES WARD
SKEET ULRICH
PUNKY BREWSTER
BARON VOLSTOCK
DOUGLAS FRASER
SCOTT GALLEY
GARY KELLEY
KWABENA PAYNE
BELINDA AGEDA
WITNESSED AND NOTARIZED
THE OFFICE OF THE MAYOR OF
BIRMINGHAM, #223-6-8898-999-7
10 MAY 1963
Within 90 days lunch counters, restrooms, fitting rooms, and drinking fountains would be desegregated.
Within 60 days Blacks would be hired in clerk, sales, and other positions previously closed to us. And communications were set up for further dialogue between the parties.
Of course, present were the usual criticisms that the accord didn't go far enough, but that was to be expected. No matter what you do ***someone's*** going to complain....
No good deed ever goes unpunished.
Emmett Till. Cynthia Wesley. Carol Robertson. Addie Mae Collins. Denise McNair. Brother Medgar Evers....
Simple common sense dictates no one should have to lose their ***lives*** defending their fundamental freedoms.
Then again...when the struggle is sufficiently mighty, sufficiently ***just...***I suppose that same common sense dictates a price must be exacted....

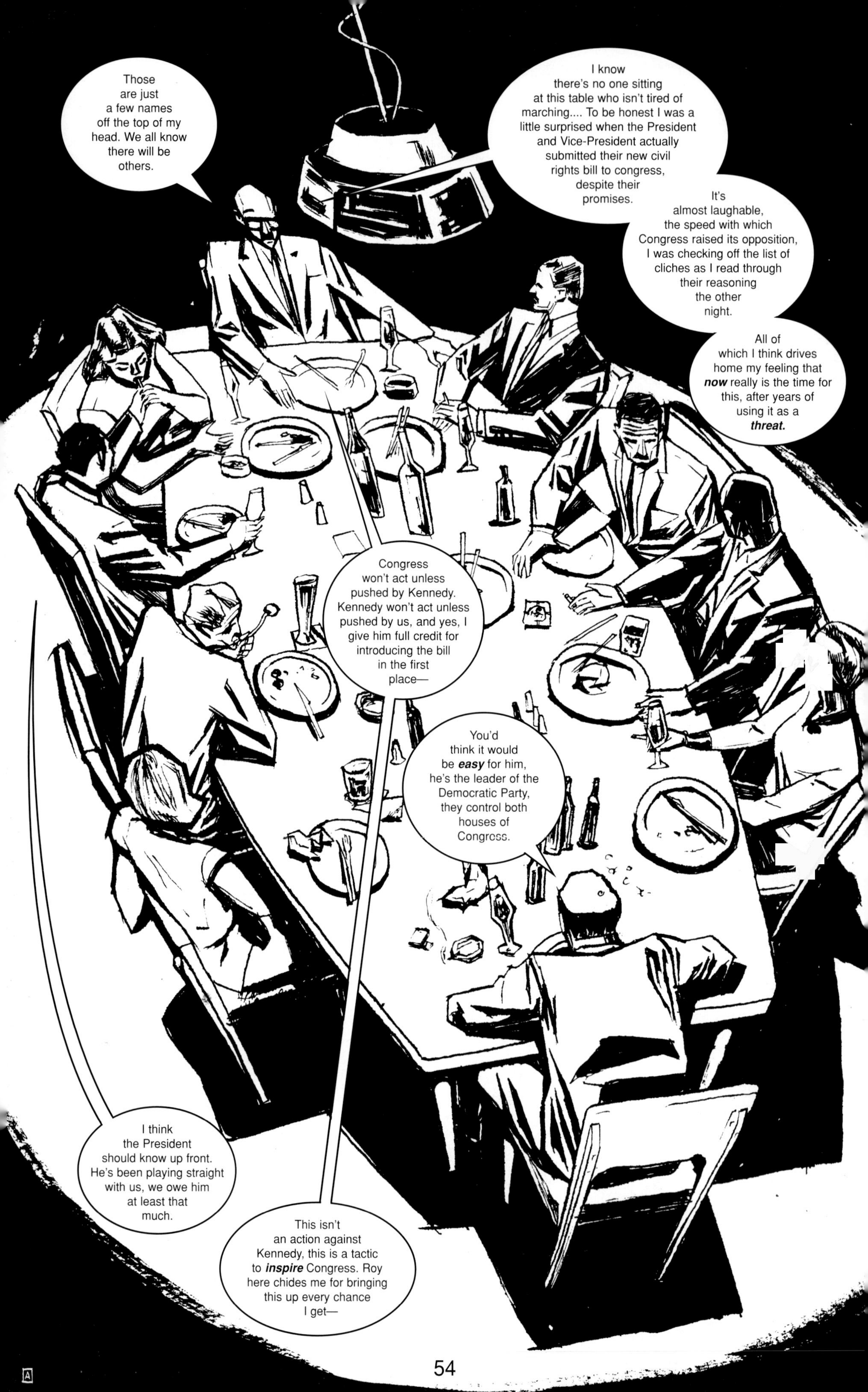
Those are just a few names off the top of my head. We all know there will be others.
I know there's no one sitting at this table who isn't tired of marching.... To be honest I was a little surprised when the President and Vice-President actually submitted their new civil rights bill to congress, despite their promises.
It's almost laughable, the speed with which Congress raised its opposition, I was checking off the list of cliches as I read through their reasoning the other night.
All of which I think drives home my feeling that *now* really is the time for this, after years of using it as a *threat.*
Congress won't act unless pushed by Kennedy. Kennedy won't act unless pushed by us, and yes, I give him full credit for introducing the bill in the first place—
You'd think it would be *easy* for him, he's the leader of the Democratic Party, they control both houses of Congress.
I think the President should know up front. He's been playing straight with us, we owe him at least that much.
This isn't an action against Kennedy, this is a tactic to *inspire* Congress. Roy here chides me for bringing this up every chance I get—

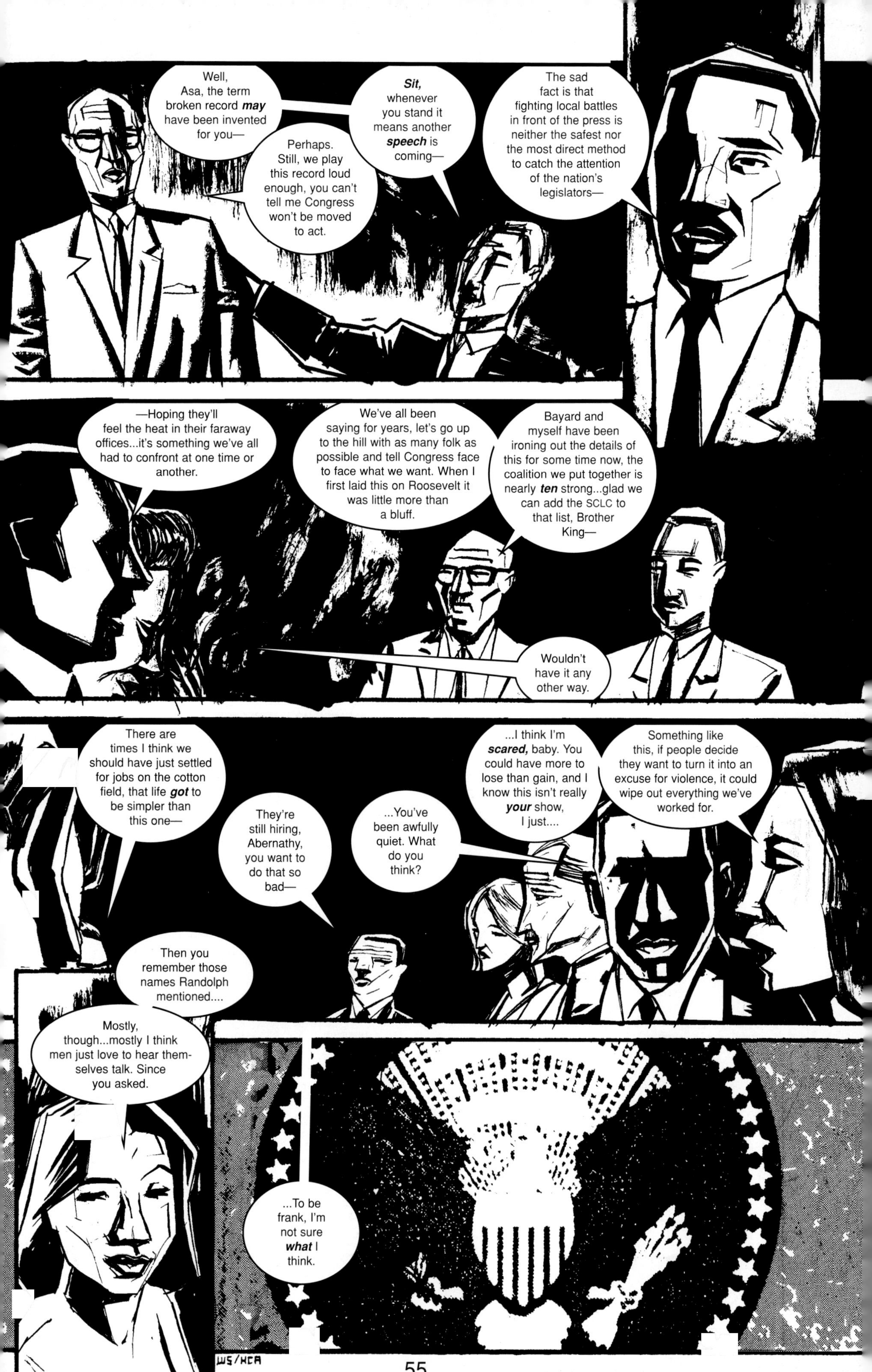
Well, Asa, the term broken record **may** have been invented for you—
Perhaps. Still, we play this record loud enough, you can't tell me Congress won't be moved to act.
Sit, whenever you stand it means another ***speech*** is coming—
The sad fact is that fighting local battles in front of the press is neither the safest nor the most direct method to catch the attention of the nation's legislators—
—Hoping they'll feel the heat in their faraway offices...it's something we've all had to confront at one time or another.
We've all been saying for years, let's go up to the hill with as many folk as possible and tell Congress face to face what we want. When I first laid this on Roosevelt it was little more than a bluff.
Bayard and myself have been ironing out the details of this for some time now, the coalition we put together is nearly ***ten*** strong...glad we can add the SCLC to that list, Brother King—
Wouldn't have it any other way.
There are times I think we should have just settled for jobs on the cotton field, that life ***got*** to be simpler than this one—
They're still hiring, Abernathy, you want to do that so bad—
...You've been awfully quiet. What do you think?
...I think I'm ***scared,*** baby. You could have more to lose than gain, and I know this isn't really ***your*** show, I just....
Something like this, if people decide they want to turn it into an excuse for violence, it could wipe out everything we've worked for.
Then you remember those names Randolph mentioned....
Mostly, though...mostly I think men just love to hear themselves talk. Since you asked.
...To be frank, I'm not sure ***what*** I think.
WS/HCA

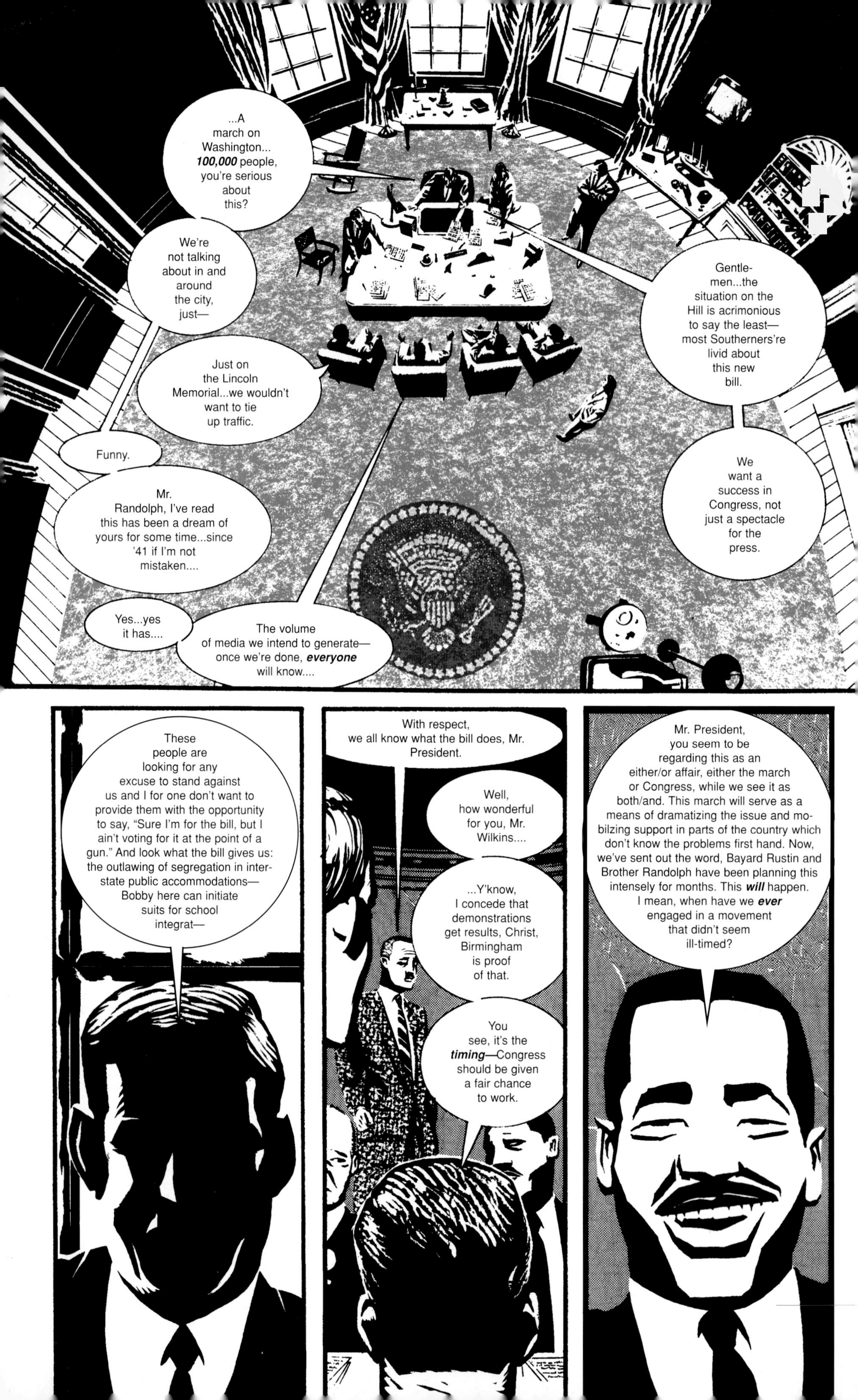
...A march on Washington... ***100,000*** people, you're serious about this?
We're not talking about in and around the city, just—
Just on the Lincoln Memorial...we wouldn't want to tie up traffic.
Funny.
Mr. Randolph, I've read this has been a dream of yours for some time...since '41 if I'm not mistaken....
Yes...yes it has....
The volume of media we intend to generate— once we're done, ***everyone*** will know....
Gentle-men...the situation on the Hill is acrimonious to say the least— most Southerners're livid about this new bill.
We want a success in Congress, not just a spectacle for the press.
These people are looking for any excuse to stand against us and I for one don't want to provide them with the opportunity to say, "Sure I'm for the bill, but I ain't voting for it at the point of a gun." And look what the bill gives us: the outlawing of segregation in inter-state public accommodations— Bobby here can initiate suits for school integrat—
With respect, we all know what the bill does, Mr. President.
Well, how wonderful for you, Mr. Wilkins....
...Y'know, I concede that demonstrations get results, Christ, Birmingham is proof of that.
You see, it's the ***timing***—Congress should be given a fair chance to work.
Mr. President, you seem to be regarding this as an either/or affair, either the march or Congress, while we see it as both/and. This march will serve as a means of dramatizing the issue and mo-bilzing support in parts of the country which don't know the problems first hand. Now, we've sent out the word, Bayard Rustin and Brother Randolph have been planning this intensely for months. This ***will*** happen. I mean, when have we ***ever*** engaged in a movement that didn't seem ill-timed?

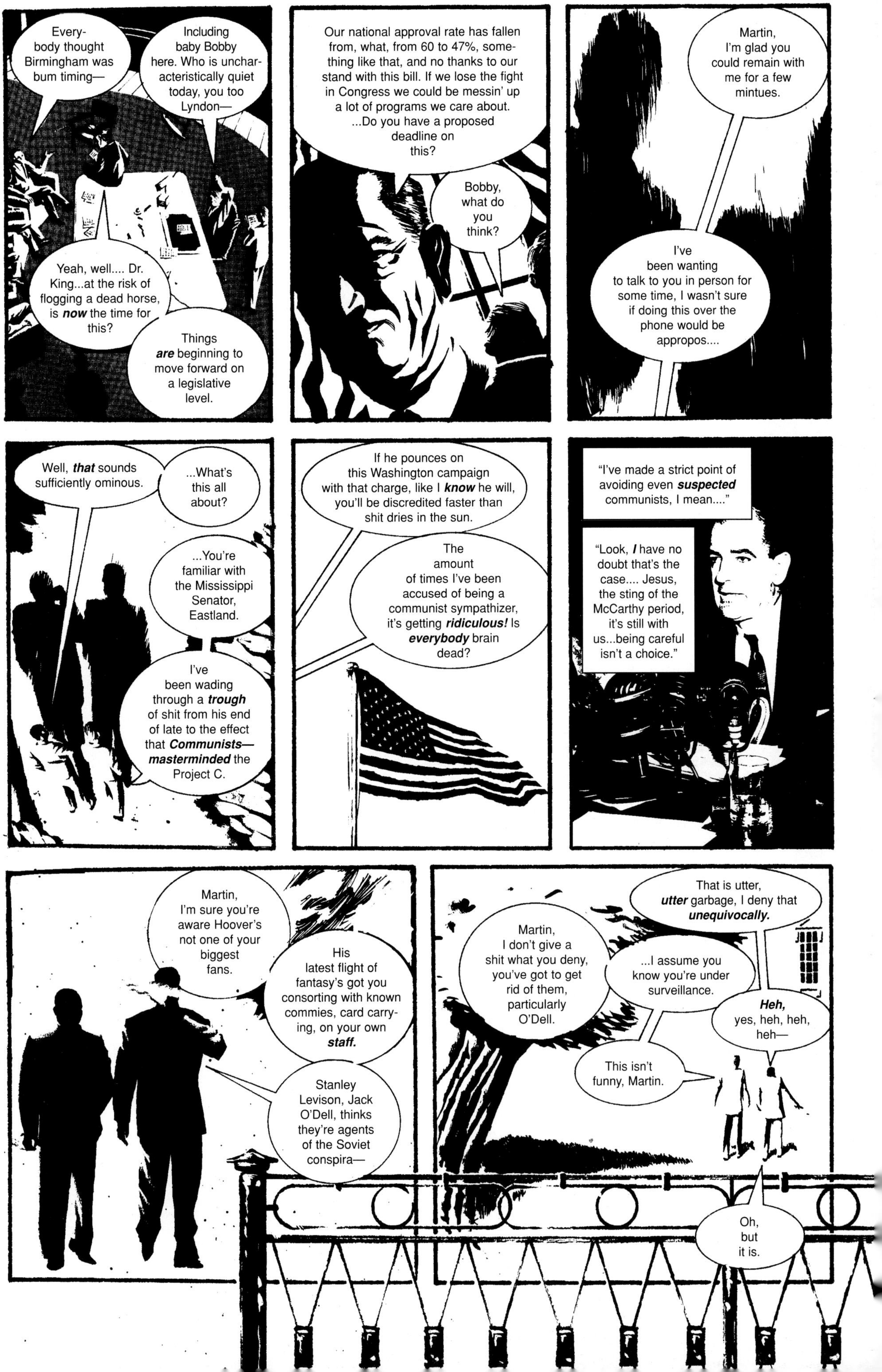

Every-body thought Birmingham was bum timing—
Including baby Bobby here. Who is uncharacteristically quiet today, you too Lyndon—
Yeah, well.... Dr. King...at the risk of flogging a dead horse, is *now* the time for this?
Things *are* beginning to move forward on a legislative level.
Our national approval rate has fallen from, what, from 60 to 47%, something like that, and no thanks to our stand with this bill. If we lose the fight in Congress we could be messin' up a lot of programs we care about. ...Do you have a proposed deadline on this?
Bobby, what do you think?
Martin, I'm glad you could remain with me for a few mintues.
I've been wanting to talk to you in person for some time, I wasn't sure if doing this over the phone would be appropos....
Well, *that* sounds sufficiently ominous.
...What's this all about?
...You're familiar with the Mississippi Senator, Eastland.
I've been wading through a *trough* of shit from his end of late to the effect that *Communists—masterminded* the Project C.
If he pounces on this Washington campaign with that charge, like I *know* he will, you'll be discredited faster than shit dries in the sun.
The amount of times I've been accused of being a communist sympathizer, it's getting *ridiculous!* Is *everybody* brain dead?
"I've made a strict point of avoiding even *suspected* communists, I mean...."
"Look, *I* have no doubt that's the case.... Jesus, the sting of the McCarthy period, it's still with us...being careful isn't a choice."
Martin, I'm sure you're aware Hoover's not one of your biggest fans.
His latest flight of fantasy's got you consorting with known commies, card carrying, on your own *staff.*
Stanley Levison, Jack O'Dell, thinks they're agents of the Soviet conspira—
That is utter, *utter* garbage, I deny that *unequivocally.*
Martin, I don't give a shit what you deny, you've got to get rid of them, particularly O'Dell.
...I assume you know you're under surveillance.
Heh, yes, heh, heh, heh—
This isn't funny, Martin.
Oh, but it is.

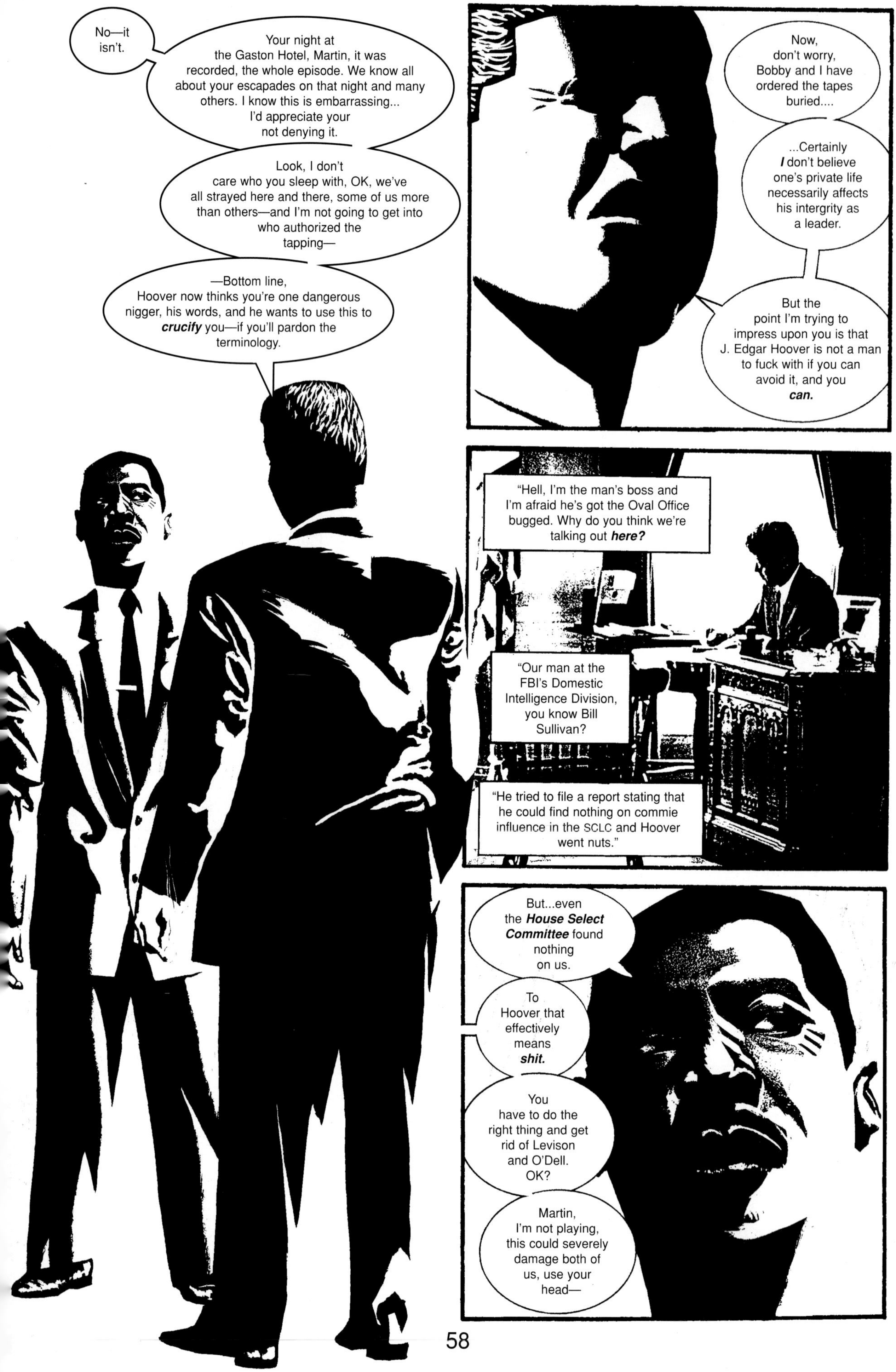

No—it isn't.
Your night at the Gaston Hotel, Martin, it was recorded, the whole episode. We know all about your escapades on that night and many others. I know this is embarrassing... I'd appreciate your not denying it.
Look, I don't care who you sleep with, OK, we've all strayed here and there, some of us more than others—and I'm not going to get into who authorized the tapping—
—Bottom line, Hoover now thinks you're one dangerous nigger, his words, and he wants to use this to ***crucify*** you—if you'll pardon the terminology.
Now, don't worry, Bobby and I have ordered the tapes buried....
...Certainly ***I*** don't believe one's private life necessarily affects his intergrity as a leader.
But the point I'm trying to impress upon you is that J. Edgar Hoover is not a man to fuck with if you can avoid it, and you ***can.***
"Hell, I'm the man's boss and I'm afraid he's got the Oval Office bugged. Why do you think we're talking out ***here?***
"Our man at the FBI's Domestic Intelligence Division, you know Bill Sullivan?
"He tried to file a report stating that he could find nothing on commie influence in the SCLC and Hoover went nuts."
But...even the ***House Select Committee*** found nothing on us.
To Hoover that effectively means ***shit.***
You have to do the right thing and get rid of Levison and O'Dell. OK?
Martin, I'm not playing, this could severely damage both of us, use your head—

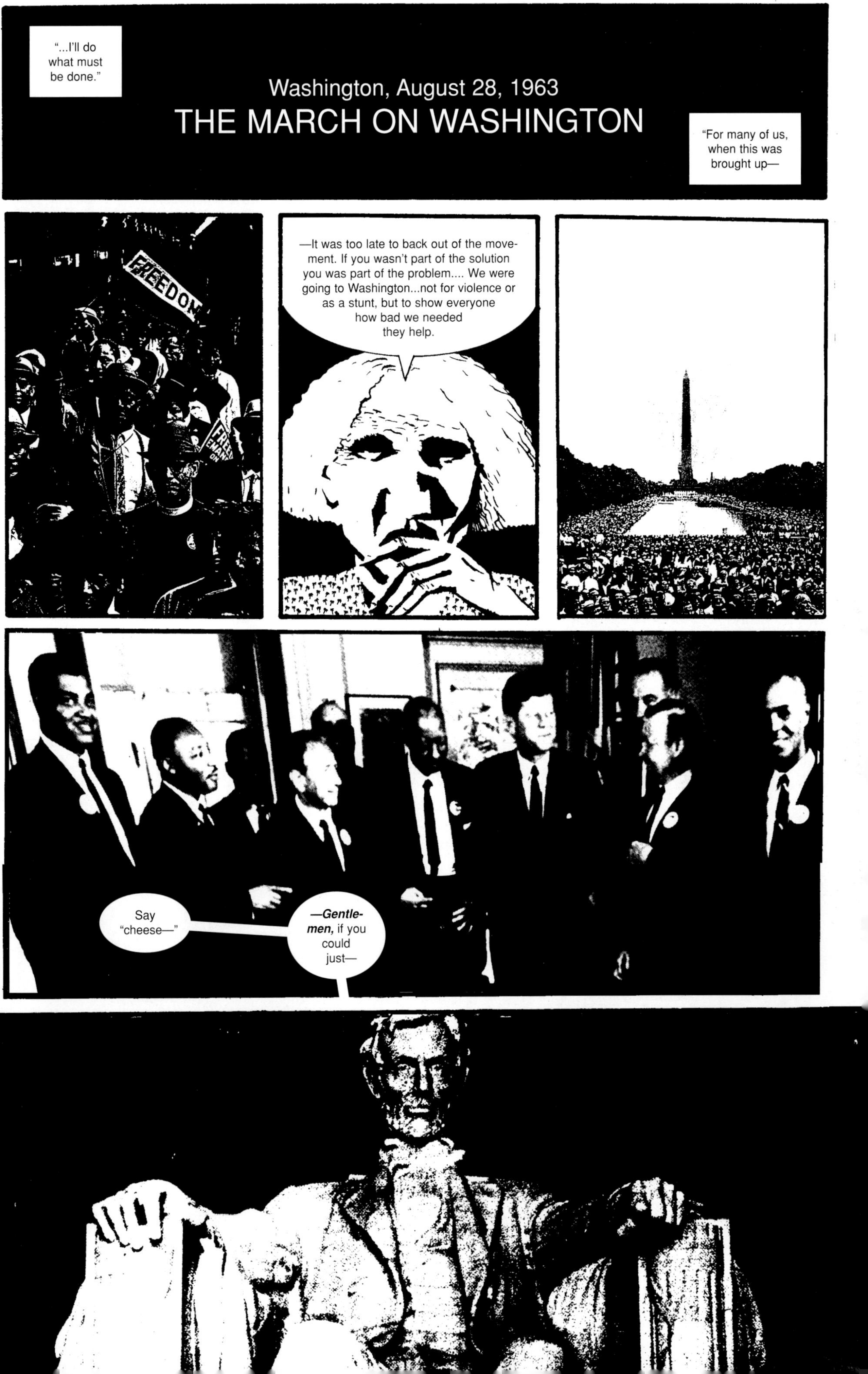
"...I'll do what must be done."
Washington, August 28, 1963
THE MARCH ON WASHINGTON
"For many of us, when this was brought up—
FREEDOM
—It was too late to back out of the movement. If you wasn't part of the solution you was part of the problem.... We were going to Washington...not for violence or as a stunt, but to show everyone how bad we needed they help.
Say "cheese—"
—Gentlemen, if you could just—

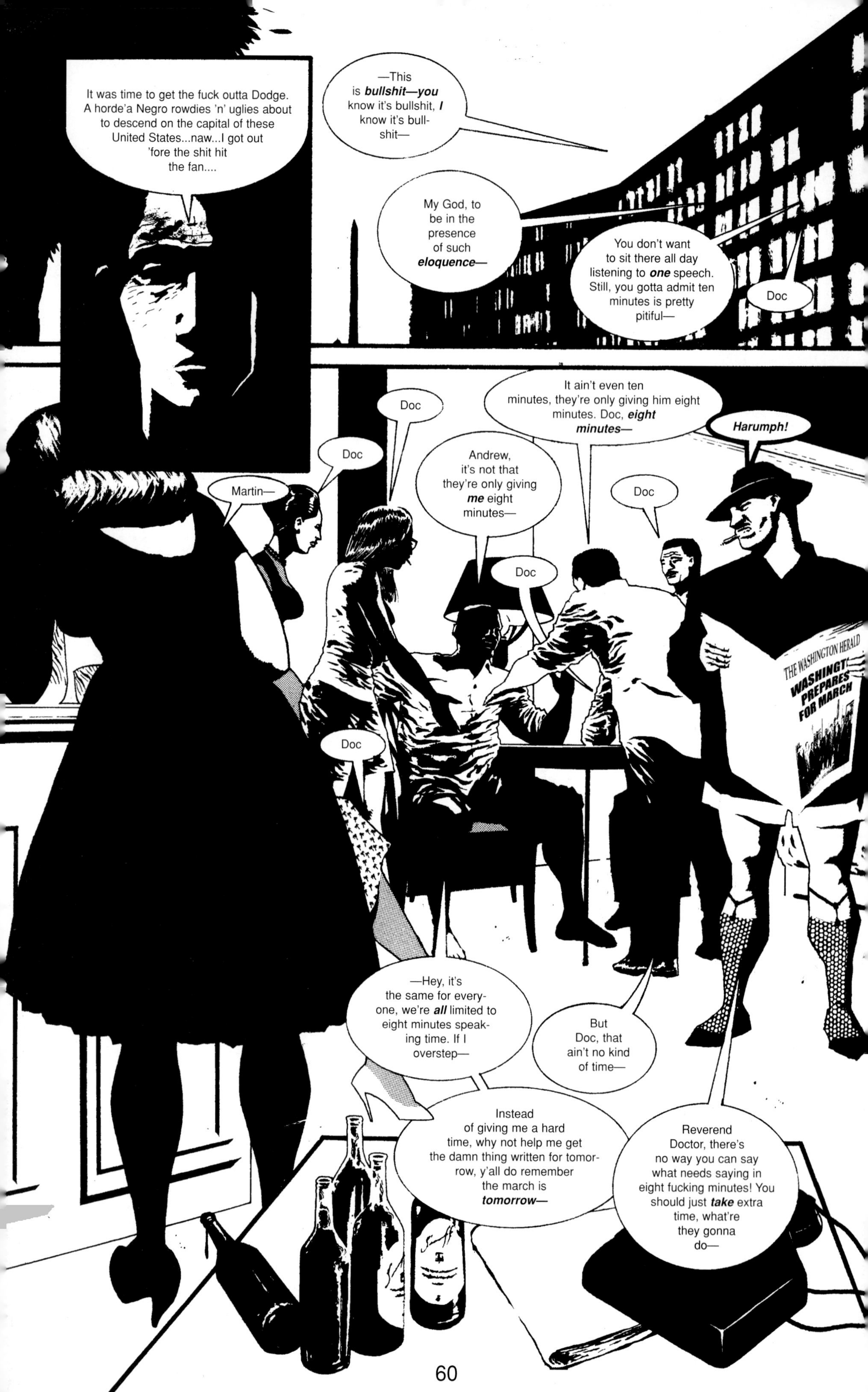
It was time to get the fuck outta Dodge. A horde'a Negro rowdies 'n' uglies about to descend on the capital of these United States...naw...I got out 'fore the shit hit the fan....
—This is ***bullshit—you*** know it's bullshit, ***I*** know it's bull-shit—
My God, to be in the presence of such ***eloquence***—
You don't want to sit there all day listening to ***one*** speech. Still, you gotta admit ten minutes is pretty pitiful—
Doc
Doc
It ain't even ten minutes, they're only giving him eight minutes. Doc, ***eight minutes***—
Harumph!
Doc
Andrew, it's not that they're only giving ***me*** eight minutes—
Martin—
Doc
Doc
THE WASHINGTON HERALD
WASHINGT
PREPARES FOR MARCH
Doc
—Hey, it's the same for every-one, we're ***all*** limited to eight minutes speak-ing time. If I overstep—
But Doc, that ain't no kind of time—
Instead of giving me a hard time, why not help me get the damn thing written for tomor-row, y'all do remember the march is ***tomorrow***—
Reverend Doctor, there's no way you can say what needs saying in eight fucking minutes! You should just ***take*** extra time, what're they gonna do—

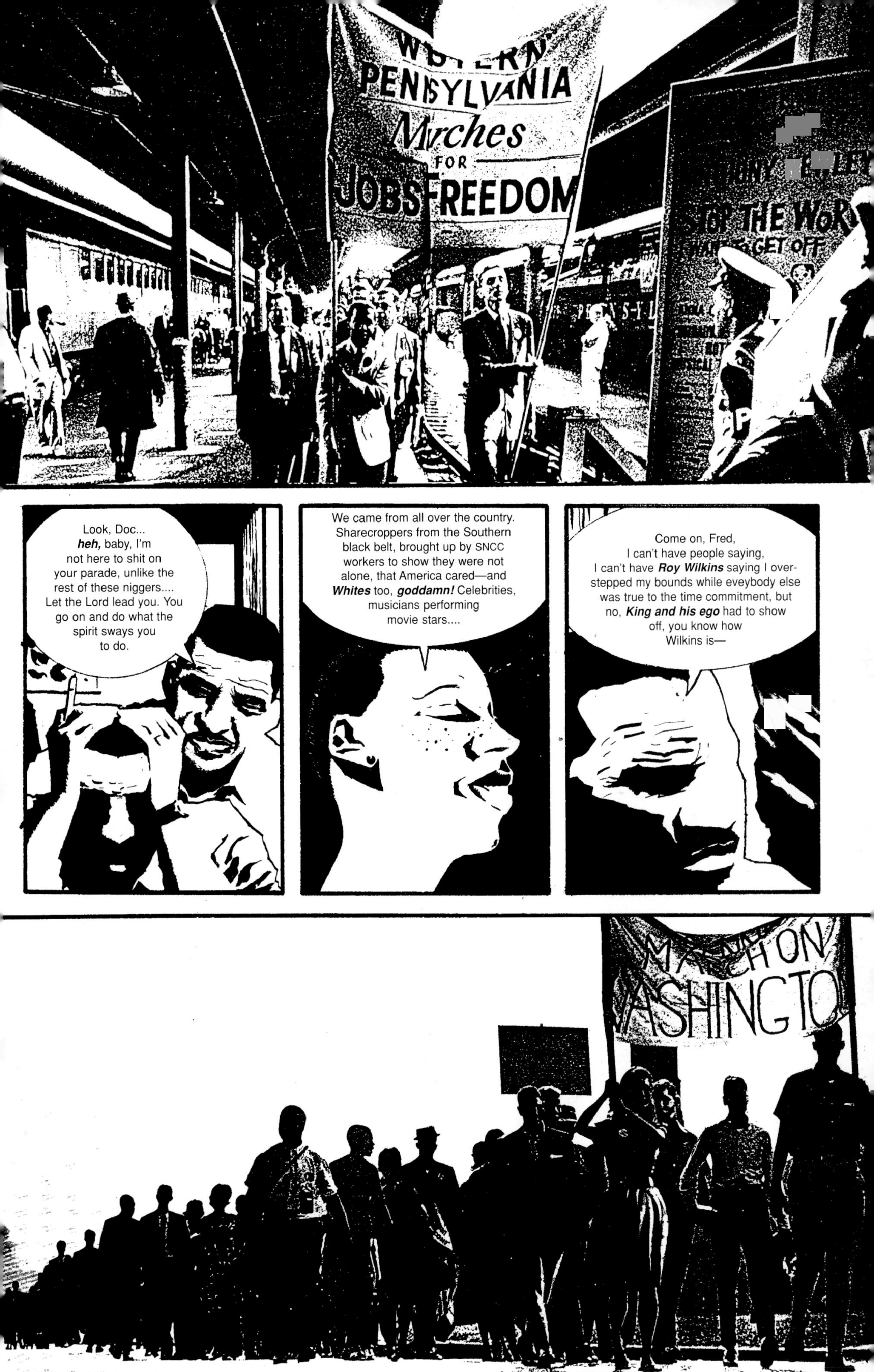
PENNSYLVANIA
FOR
JOBS FREEDOM
Look, Doc... **heh,** baby, I'm not here to shit on your parade, unlike the rest of these niggers.... Let the Lord lead you. You go on and do what the spirit sways you to do.
We came from all over the country. Sharecroppers from the Southern black belt, brought up by SNCC workers to show they were not alone, that America cared—and ***Whites*** too, ***goddamn!*** Celebrities, musicians performing movie stars....
Come on, Fred, I can't have people saying, I can't have ***Roy Wilkins*** saying I over-stepped my bounds while eveybody else was true to the time commitment, but no, ***King and his ego*** had to show off, you know how Wilkins is—

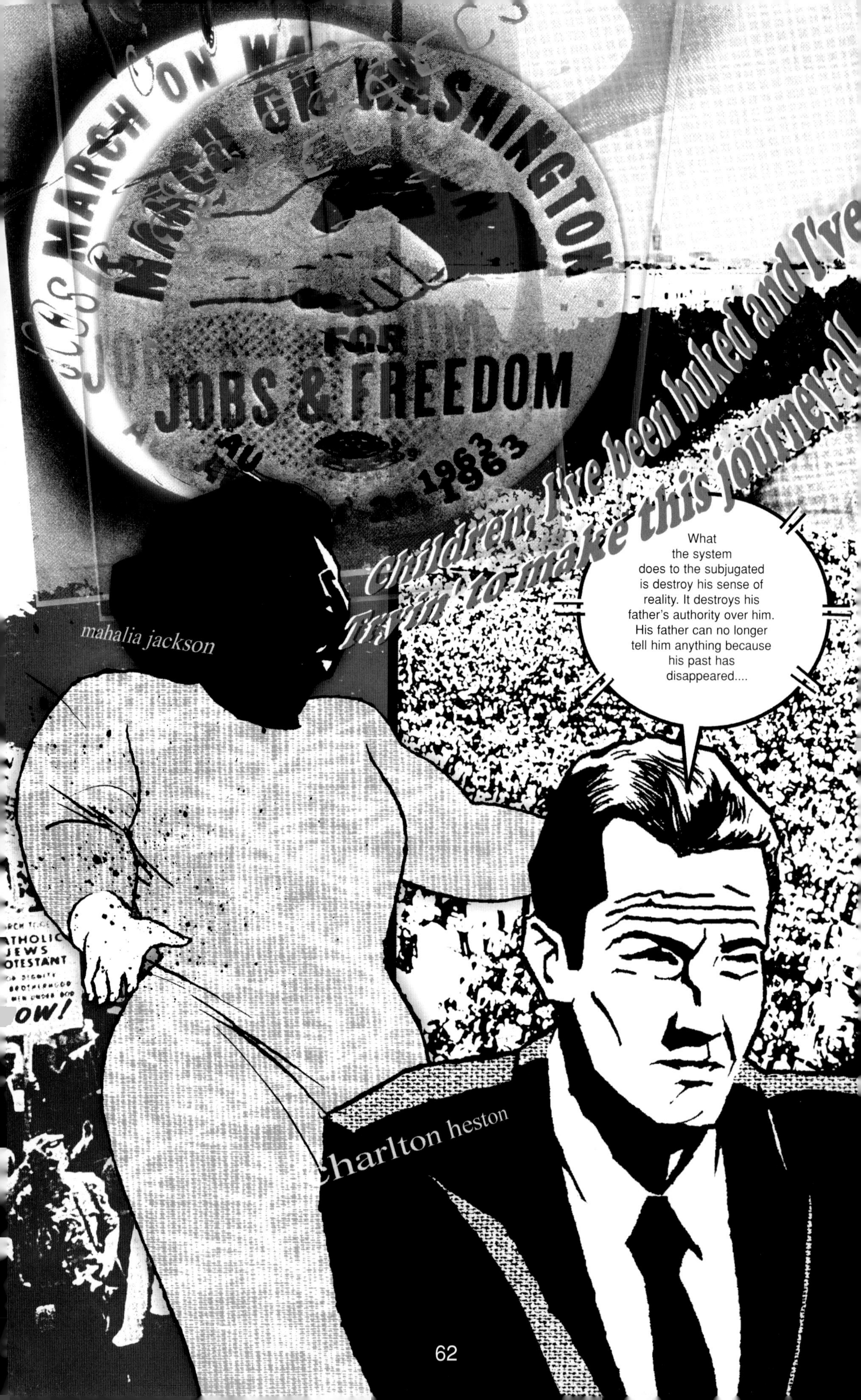

MARCH ON WASHINGTON
FOR
JOBS & FREEDOM
1963
Children, I've been buked and I've
Tryin' to make this journey al
mahalia jackson
What the system does to the subjugated is destroy his sense of reality. It destroys his father's authority over him. His father can no longer tell him anything because his past has disappeared....
ATHOLIC
JEWS
OTESTANT
OW!
charlton heston

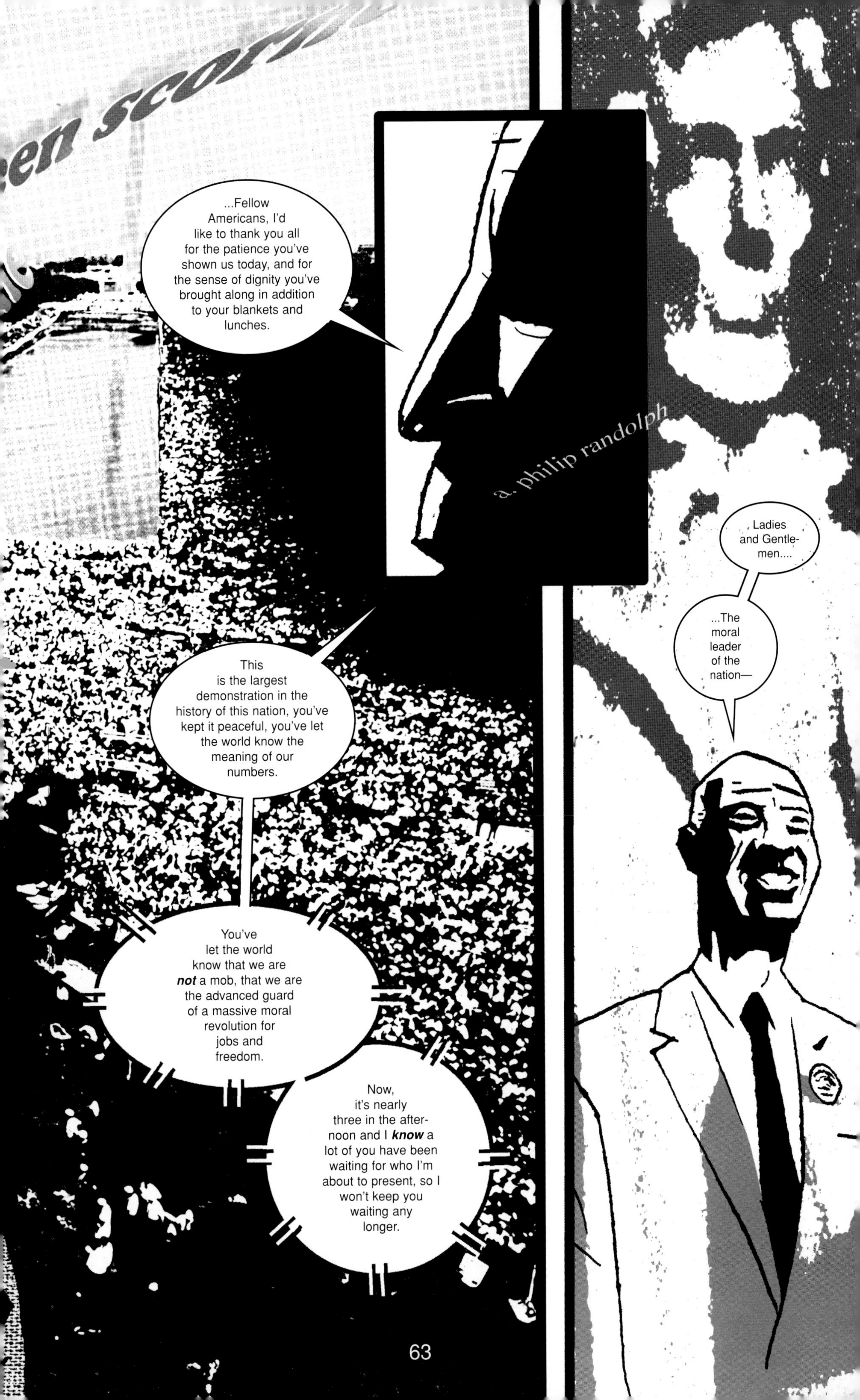
...Fellow Americans, I'd like to thank you all for the patience you've shown us today, and for the sense of dignity you've brought along in addition to your blankets and lunches.
a. philip randolph
This is the largest demonstration in the history of this nation, you've kept it peaceful, you've let the world know the meaning of our numbers.
You've let the world know that we are ***not*** a mob, that we are the advanced guard of a massive moral revolution for jobs and freedom.
Now, it's nearly three in the after-noon and I ***know*** a lot of you have been waiting for who I'm about to present, so I won't keep you waiting any longer.
Ladies and Gentle-men....
...The moral leader of the nation—

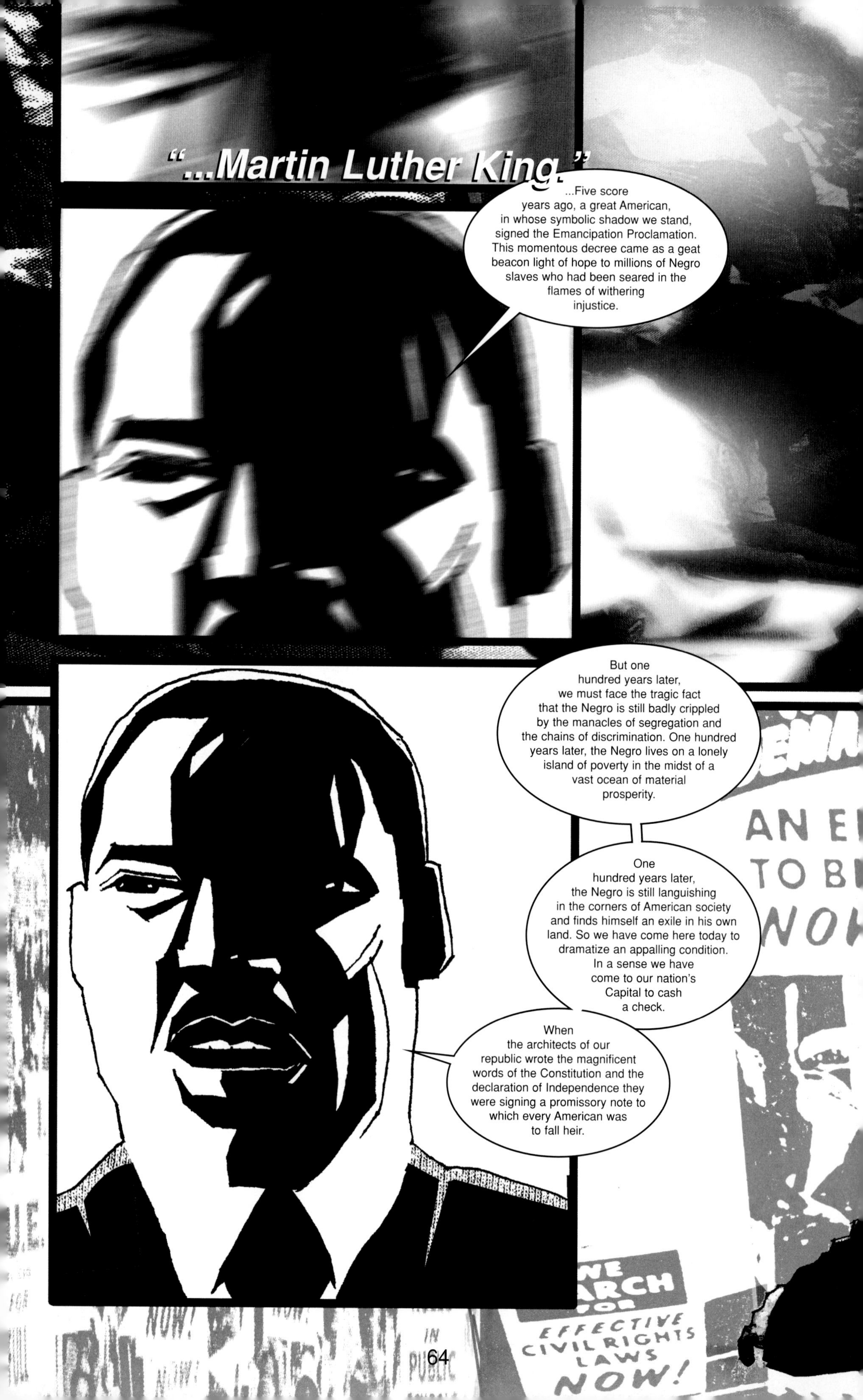
"...Martin Luther King."
...Five score years ago, a great American, in whose symbolic shadow we stand, signed the Emancipation Proclamation. This momentous decree came as a geat beacon light of hope to millions of Negro slaves who had been seared in the flames of withering injustice.
But one hundred years later, we must face the tragic fact that the Negro is still badly crippled by the manacles of segregation and the chains of discrimination. One hundred years later, the Negro lives on a lonely island of poverty in the midst of a vast ocean of material prosperity.
One hundred years later, the Negro is still languishing in the corners of American society and finds himself an exile in his own land. So we have come here today to dramatize an appalling condition. In a sense we have come to our nation's Capital to cash a check.
When the architects of our republic wrote the magnificent words of the Constitution and the declaration of Independence they were signing a promissory note to which every American was to fall heir.
EFFECTIVE CIVIL RIGHTS LAWS NOW!

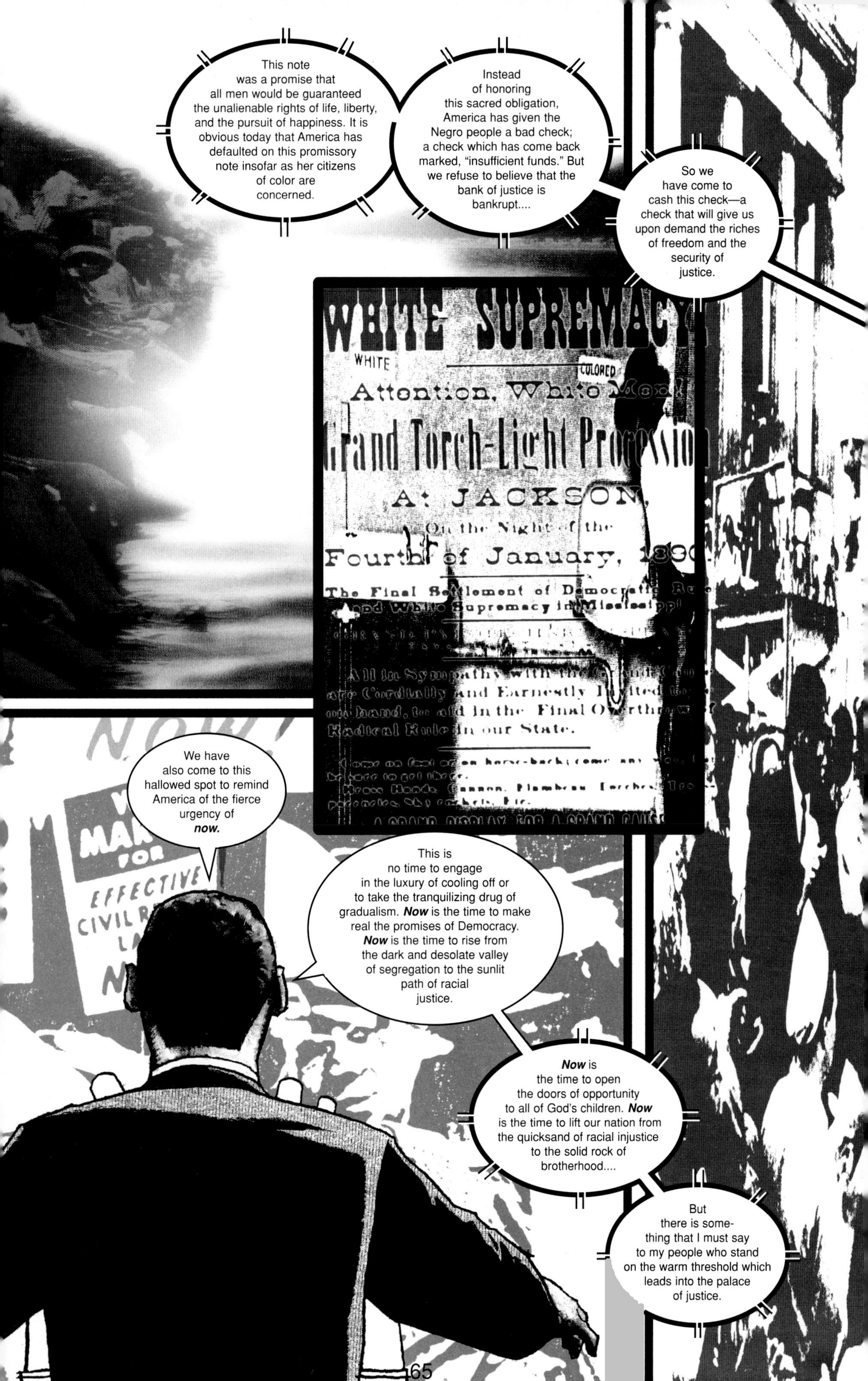
This note was a promise that all men would be guaranteed the unalienable rights of life, liberty, and the pursuit of happiness. It is obvious today that America has defaulted on this promissory note insofar as her citizens of color are concerned.
Instead of honoring this sacred obligation, America has given the Negro people a bad check; a check which has come back marked, "insufficient funds." But we refuse to believe that the bank of justice is bankrupt....
So we have come to cash this check—a check that will give us upon demand the riches of freedom and the security of justice.
WHITE SUPREMACY
WHITE
COLORED
JACKSON
Fourth of January,
We have also come to this hallowed spot to remind America of the fierce urgency of *now.*
EFFECTIVE
This is no time to engage in the luxury of cooling off or to take the tranquilizing drug of gradualism. ***Now*** is the time to make real the promises of Democracy. ***Now*** is the time to rise from the dark and desolate valley of segregation to the sunlit path of racial justice.
Now is the time to open the doors of opportunity to all of God's children. ***Now*** is the time to lift our nation from the quicksand of racial injustice to the solid rock of brotherhood....
But there is something that I must say to my people who stand on the warm threshold which leads into the palace of justice.

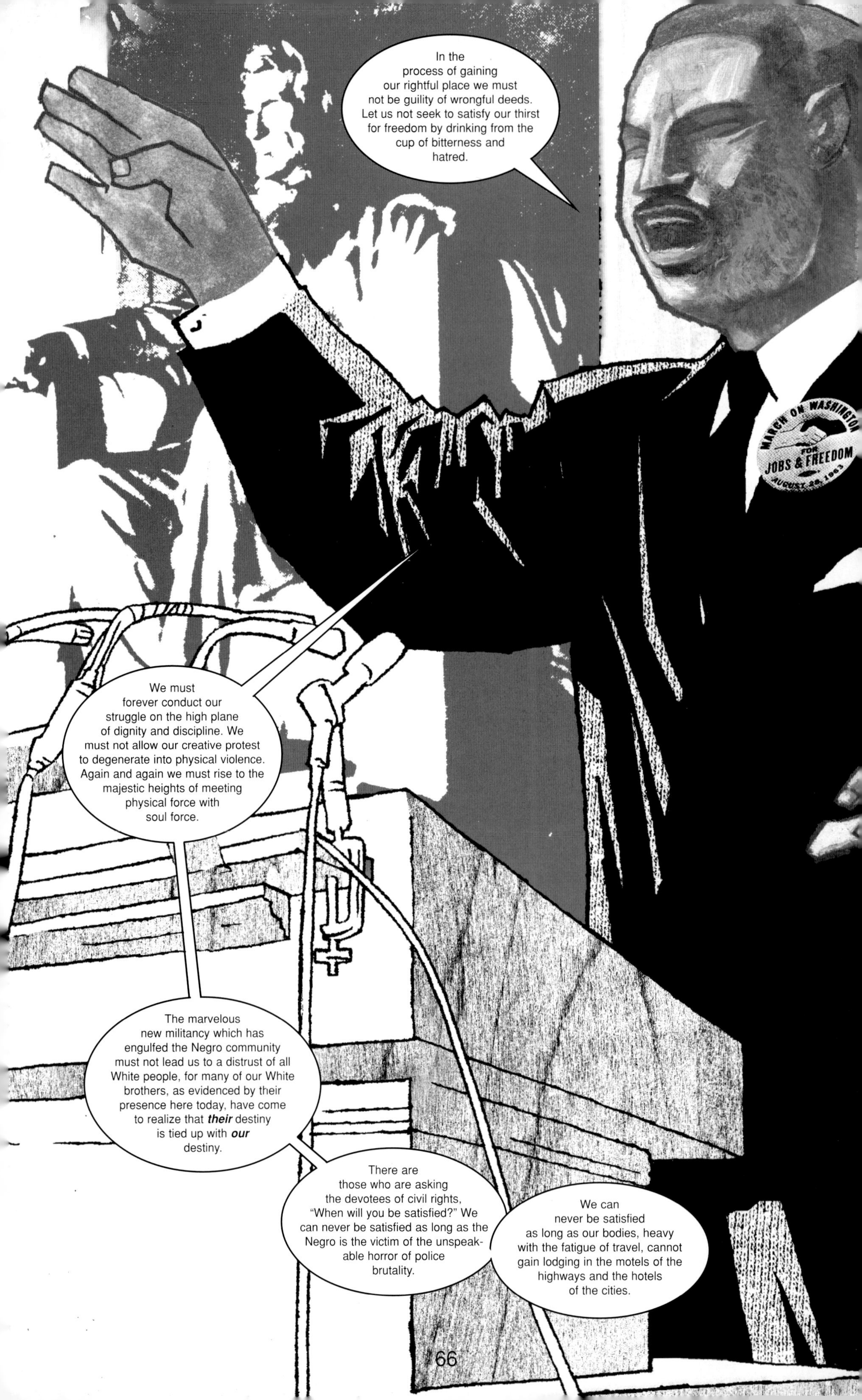
In the process of gaining our rightful place we must not be guility of wrongful deeds. Let us not seek to satisfy our thirst for freedom by drinking from the cup of bitterness and hatred.
MARCH ON WASHINGTON FOR JOBS & FREEDOM AUGUST 28, 1963
We must forever conduct our struggle on the high plane of dignity and discipline. We must not allow our creative protest to degenerate into physical violence. Again and again we must rise to the majestic heights of meeting physical force with soul force.
The marvelous new militancy which has engulfed the Negro community must not lead us to a distrust of all White people, for many of our White brothers, as evidenced by their presence here today, have come to realize that ***their*** destiny is tied up with ***our*** destiny.
There are those who are asking the devotees of civil rights, "When will you be satisfied?" We can never be satisfied as long as the Negro is the victim of the unspeakable horror of police brutality.
We can never be satisfied as long as our bodies, heavy with the fatigue of travel, cannot gain lodging in the motels of the highways and the hotels of the cities.

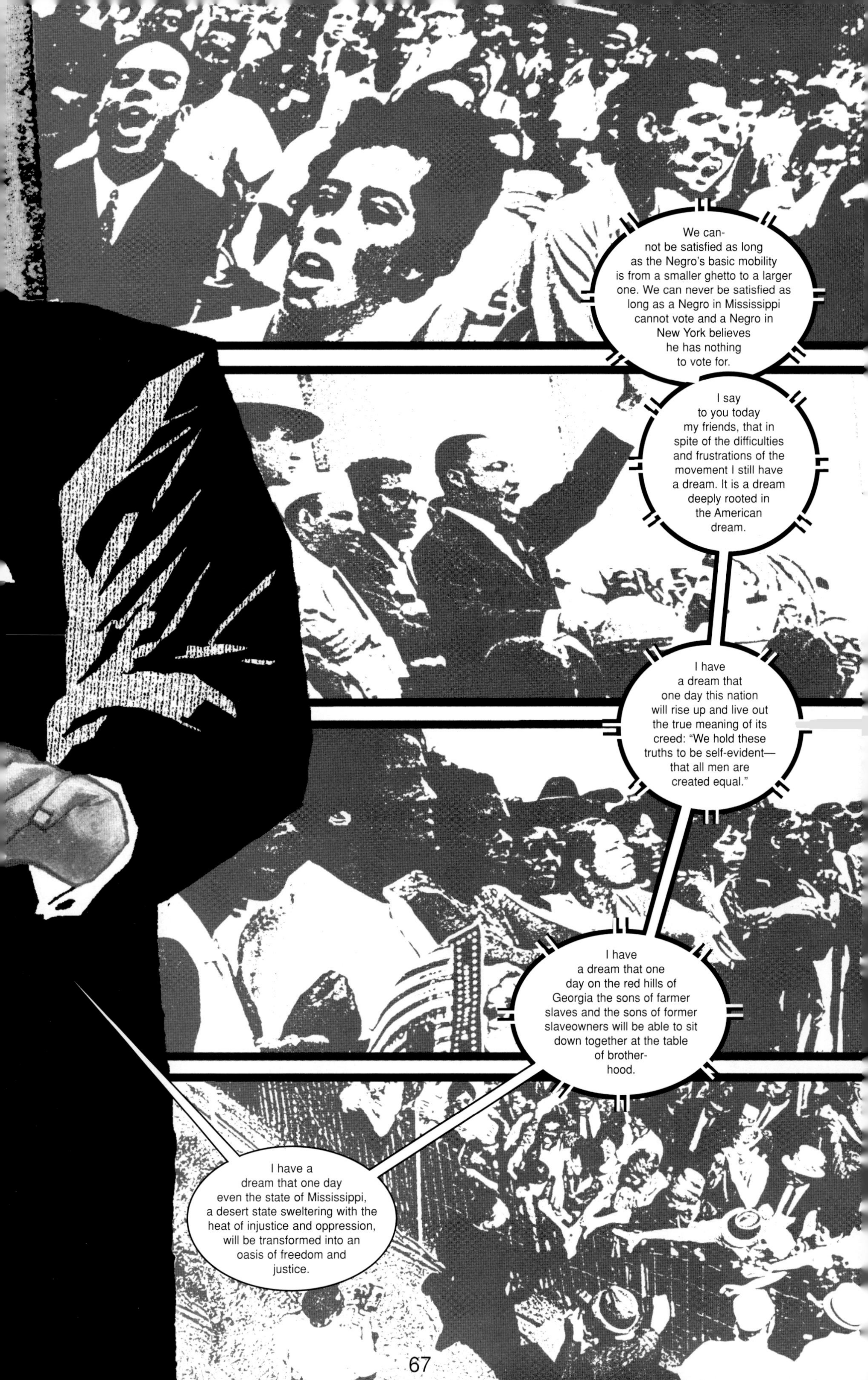

We can-not be satisfied as long as the Negro's basic mobility is from a smaller ghetto to a larger one. We can never be satisfied as long as a Negro in Mississippi cannot vote and a Negro in New York believes he has nothing to vote for.
I say to you today my friends, that in spite of the difficulties and frustrations of the movement I still have a dream. It is a dream deeply rooted in the American dream.
I have a dream that one day this nation will rise up and live out the true meaning of its creed: "We hold these truths to be self-evident—that all men are created equal."
I have a dream that one day on the red hills of Georgia the sons of farmer slaves and the sons of former slaveowners will be able to sit down together at the table of brother-hood.
I have a dream that one day even the state of Mississippi, a desert state sweltering with the heat of injustice and oppression, will be transformed into an oasis of freedom and justice.

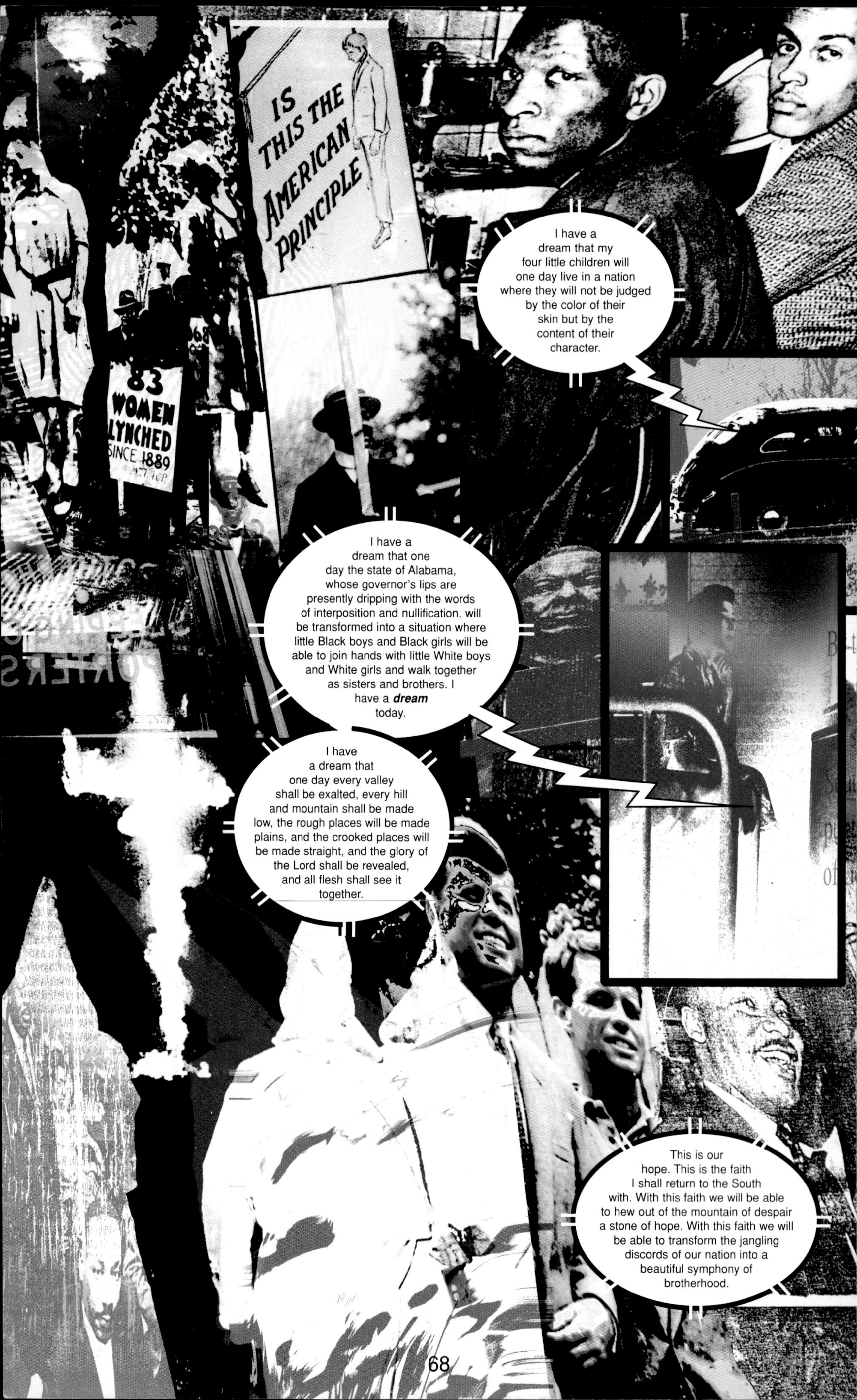
IS THIS THE AMERICAN PRINCIPLE
83 WOMEN LYNCHED SINCE 1889
I have a dream that my four little children will one day live in a nation where they will not be judged by the color of their skin but by the content of their character.
I have a dream that one day the state of Alabama, whose governor's lips are presently dripping with the words of interposition and nullification, will be transformed into a situation where little Black boys and Black girls will be able to join hands with little White boys and White girls and walk together as sisters and brothers. I have a ***dream*** today.
I have a dream that one day every valley shall be exalted, every hill and mountain shall be made low, the rough places will be made plains, and the crooked places will be made straight, and the glory of the Lord shall be revealed, and all flesh shall see it together.
This is our hope. This is the faith I shall return to the South with. With this faith we will be able to hew out of the mountain of despair a stone of hope. With this faith we will be able to transform the jangling discords of our nation into a beautiful symphony of brotherhood.

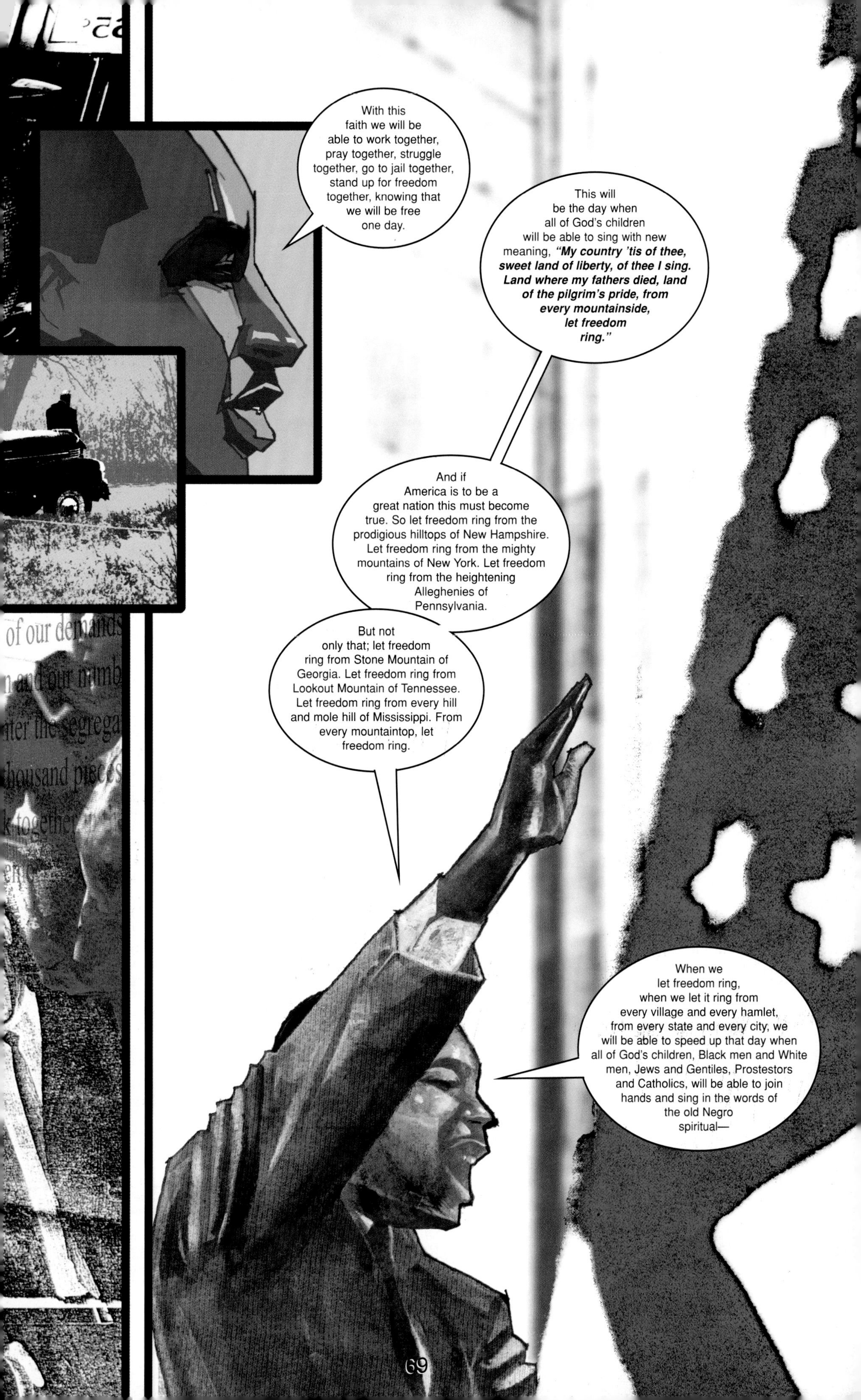
With this faith we will be able to work together, pray together, struggle together, go to jail together, stand up for freedom together, knowing that we will be free one day.
This will be the day when all of God's children will be able to sing with new meaning, ***"My country 'tis of thee, sweet land of liberty, of thee I sing. Land where my fathers died, land of the pilgrim's pride, from every mountainside, let freedom ring."***
And if America is to be a great nation this must become true. So let freedom ring from the prodigious hilltops of New Hampshire. Let freedom ring from the mighty mountains of New York. Let freedom ring from the heightening Allegheníes of Pennsylvania.
But not only that; let freedom ring from Stone Mountain of Georgia. Let freedom ring from Lookout Mountain of Tennessee. Let freedom ring from every hill and mole hill of Mississippi. From every mountaintop, let freedom ring.
When we let freedom ring, when we let it ring from every village and every hamlet, from every state and every city, we will be able to speed up that day when all of God's children, Black men and White men, Jews and Gentiles, Prostestors and Catholics, will be able to join hands and sing in the words of the old Negro spiritual—

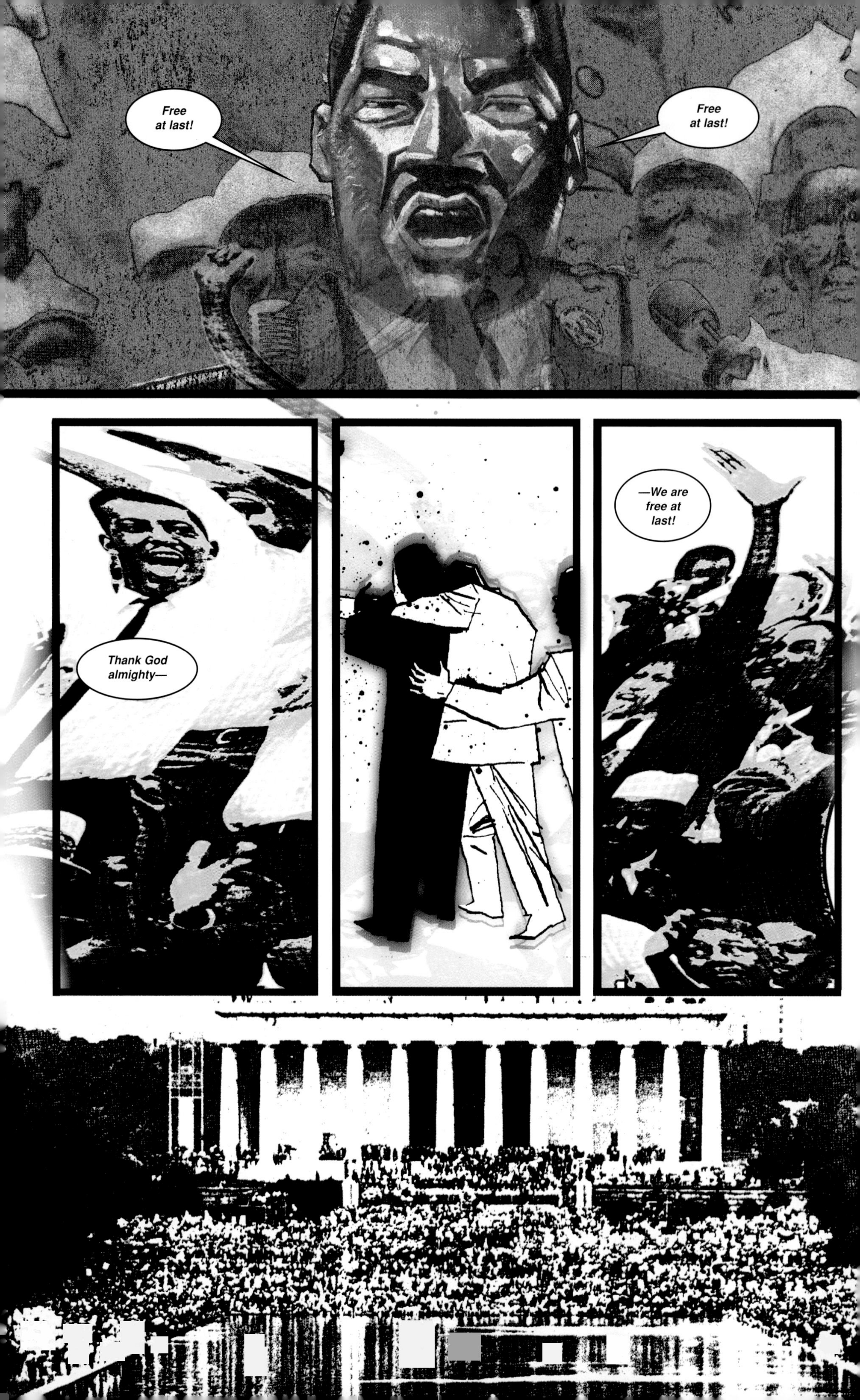
Free at last!
Free at last!
Thank God almighty—
—We are free at last!

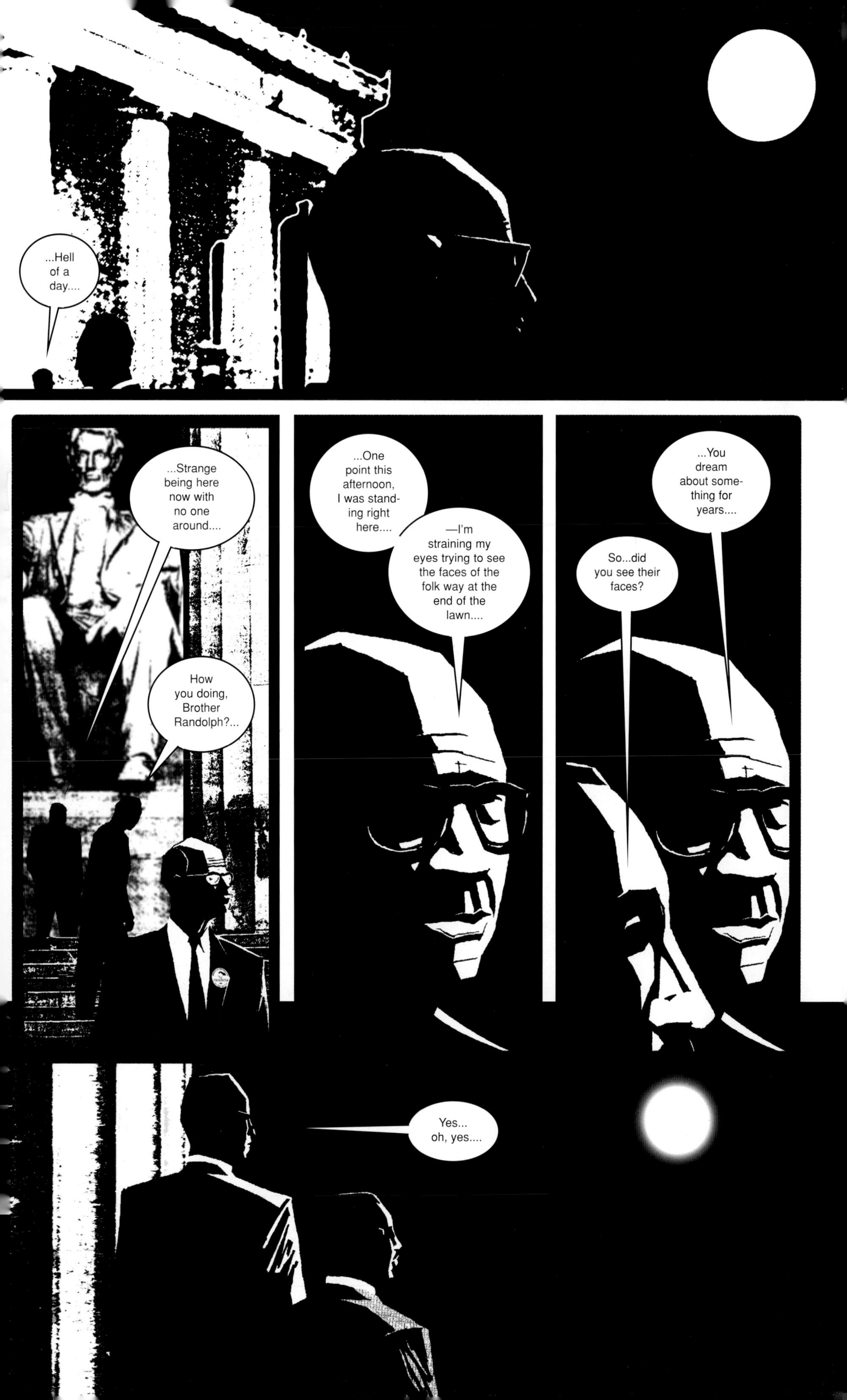
...Hell of a day....
...Strange being here now with no one around....
How you doing, Brother Randolph?...
...One point this afternoon, I was stand-ing right here....
—I'm straining my eyes trying to see the faces of the folk way at the end of the lawn....
...You dream about some-thing for years....
So...did you see their faces?
Yes... oh, yes....

NEXT:

1966-1968